Senior
Business
Studies
for New Zealand

Lloyd
Gutteridge

NELSON
CENGAGE Learning™

Australia • Brazil • Japan • Korea • Mexico • Singapore • Spain • United Kingdom • United States

Senior Business Studies
1st Edition
Lloyd Gutteridge

Cover design: Book Design Ltd
Text designer: Book Design Ltd
Production controller: Siew Han Ong
Reprint: Jess Lovell

Any URLs contained in this publication were checked for currency during the production process. Note, however, that the publisher cannot vouch for the ongoing currency of URLs.

Acknowledgements
The authors and publishers wish to think the following people and organisations for permission to use the resources in this textbook. Every effort has been made to trace and acknowledge all copyright owners of material used in this book. In most cases this was successful and copyright is acknowledged as requested. However, if any infringement has occurred the publishers tender their apologies and invite the copyright holders to contact them.

Page 14 , logos courtesy of Binary Star and Huffer; page 18, photograph courtesy of Westpac New; page 49, photographs of student army courtesy of Sam Johnson and Photographic Services Communications and Development Department, University of Canterbury; pages 54 and 56, photographs courtesy of Tasty Pot; page 55, photograph and logo courtesy of Dawn Raid Entertainment; Page 115, logo courtesy of Hell Pizza New Zealand; page 162, article courtesy of Google; page 189 Whale-watching company wins Virgin Holidays Responsible Tourism award courtesy of The Independent; page 134, diagram courtesy of Sanford Limited; articles on pages 29, 31, 37, 38, 44, 49, 54, 69, 78, 80, 87, 96, 104, 114, 115, 122, 150, 154, 175 (photo only), 186, and 197 courtesy of the New Zealand Herald; articles on pages 52, 95 and 137 courtesy of Business Desk; article on page 143 courtesy of The Economist; articles on pages 36 and 92 courtesy of The Dominion Post and © Fairfax New Zealand Limited 2011 ; article on page 55 courtesy of Manukau Courier and © Fairfax New Zealand Limited 2011; article on page 107 courtesy of The Press and © Fairfax New Zealand Limited 2011; article on page 119 courtesy of Business Day and © Fairfax New Zealand Limited 2011; articles on pages 97, 175 and 184 courtesy of NZPA; images on pages 10, 12,15,16, 19, 20, 21, 23, 24,25, 27, 31, 32, 33, 34, 35, 36, 38, 40, 41, 44, 51, 52, 57, 60, 61, 62, 64, 65, 66, 67, 71, 73, 74, 75, 77, 80, 82, 83, 88, 89, 94, 99, 100, 102, 103, 109, 111, 112, 114, 116, 117, 118, 119, 121, 123, 124, 125, 126, 127, 129, 131, 138, 139, 142, 145, 146, 147, 148, 149, 151, 152, 153,154, 158,159, 161, 163, 164, 166, 167, 168, 169, 170, 173, 177, 178, 181, 186, 187,190, 191, 193 and 194 courtesy of Shutterstock.

For product information and technology assistance,
in Australia call **1300 790 853**;
in New Zealand call **0800 449 725**

For permission to use material from this text or product, please email
aust.permissions@cengage.com

ISBN 978 0 17 021573 2

Cengage Learning Australia
Level 7, 80 Dorcas Street
South Melbourne, Victoria Australia 3205

Cengage Learning New Zealand
Unit 4B Rosedale Office Park
331 Rosedale Road, Albany, North Shore 0632, NZ

For learning solutions, visit **cengage.com.au**

Printed in China by China Translation & Printing Services.
2 3 4 5 6 7 8 16 15 14 13 12

Contents

Acknowledgements

I would like to take this opportunity to thank a number of people who have been instrumental in helping this guide see the light of day.

- Cengage Learning and Publishing especially Jenny Thomas and Graham McEwan for their enthusiasm and support for this project.

- Nick Kearns and Steve Barnett from Unitec for their encouragement and insight into trying to shift the focus of learning business from a 'chalk and talk' approach to an experiential one. Go TXB!

- My friend and mentor, Nick Hindson from Market Share.

- Mary Kerrigan from Papatoetoe High School, Vanessa Lee and Fiona Haiko from the Asia NZ Foundation for their assistance in supplying updated case study material focusing on business opportunities for Air New Zealand in China. My thanks also to Linda Everett from Onehunga Business School who made a number of important suggestion to the first draft manuscript. They bear no responsibility for any errors.

- Mrs Patricia Mahala Hall for her assistance with proof reading the draft copies.

- Finally, to my wife Elaine and two boys Sam and Joel who once again have been wonderful in supporting me in this writing process. I expect that Sam will enjoy seeing his name in print for the second time and hopefully Joel will one day soon.

A donation from the royalties of the sale of this guide will go towards helping children with autism in New Zealand.

Lloyd Gutteridge
July 2011

Introduction

Thank you for purchasing this new guide and welcome to the study of Business. The author has avoided the use of the term 'textbook' quite deliberately. This guide should be used as a 'route-map', 'navigation device' or 'toolkit' to help students and teachers develop a new learning pathway for the study of Business in New Zealand.

Students and teachers are encouraged to use this guide in combination with the Secondary Teaching and Learning Guidelines (STLG) for Business (available at http://ssol.tki.org.nz.). As this is a new subject that is still evolving at NCEA Levels 1-3 (or Levels 6-8 in the New Zealand New Curriculum document) please check this website for regular updates to the intended learning outcomes.

How to use this guide

This guide has been written for both Level 1 and 2 students. It assumes no previous knowledge of Business but accepts that many students in New Zealand study financial literacy or commerce type courses at years 9 and 10 to prepare students for NCEA study in Accounting, Business and Economics. For this reason, detailed explanation on accounting principles or economic theory from pre-NCEA courses has been omitted to avoid any possible duplication.

Secondly, an inquiry approach to teaching and learning to build on the interests and experiences of students and (teachers!) is used wherever possible. It is the intention of the author that the guide will allow discussion in small groups around activities and an opportunity to engage in critical and creative thinking. Research exercises have also been given to allow students the opportunity to update the case study material presented.

Please note that Level 2 students without prior knowledge of Level 1 are strongly encouraged to study the communication unit, which has links to the units on leadership, motivation and organisational culture. They may also wish to consider reviewing the units on sources of finance, the importance of financial accounts and cashflow to help them with business decision-making and internal controls.

In a similar manner Level 1 students may wish to read those units that, although not explicitly linked to the Level 1 Teaching and Learning guide, provide deeper understanding of key business concepts. The units on motivation, citizenship, ethical behavior and organisational culture are good examples.

Senior Business Studies   ISBN 9780170215732

The structure of the guide

The opening units of this guide are common to both Level 1 and 2, and try to establish the nature of business activity, enterprise, innovation and risk-taking. Key concepts such as business objectives, stakeholders and the external environment follow the 'Big ideas' that are central to the study of Business. For Level 1 enterprise and sustainability. Citizenship or corporate social responsibility is added for Level 2. It is recommended that students have a firm grasp of these concepts before proceeding with the remaining units.

Features

- Theoretical business content and explanations have been kept to a minimum. In our knowledge-rich world accessible by the Internet, theoretical content and definitions are only a Google away. Students are encouraged to work in groups and share their knowledge of key terms which is a core competency of the new New Zealand Curriculum.

- In addition to the 27 units of teaching and learning material, four additional case studies have been given. These have been written to provide an engaging context to study some challenging issues such as sustainability and globalisation. It is hoped that they will provoke discussion, debate and the sharing of ideas in class.

- Previous examination questions from 2010 for Level 1 and sample Level 2 questions have been given at the end of the guide to maintain an assessment focus for External Achievement Standards.

A final note about using case studies

At every available opportunity, New Zealand and international case studies have been used in order to provide an engaging setting or context for the business ideas and concepts being discussed.

The case study material is provided as a stimulus or prompt to allow students and teachers to discuss some of the issues or problems that may arise. Some activities can be undertaken in class with the support of ICT, or in the case of Research or Thinking activities in small groups.

The material in each case study is designed to engage and create opportunities for the discussion of business decision-making. Students should not try to seek out the bit of the case study which gives them the 'right answer.'

Business activity in New Zealand

At the end of this unit you will be able to:

- Define what a business is and why business activity is needed to satisfy needs and wants.
- Identify important trends around the size of New Zealand businesses.
- Understand the cultural make-up of New Zealand and why we need to incorporate this into our understanding about New Zealand business.

What is a business?

That is not an easy question to answer. One definition could be …

Definition

A **business** is an entity that tries to combine human, physical and financial resources to produce goods or services that respond to and satisfy customer needs.

The Internet has changed many aspects of our lives and one significant impact has been the changing nature of what exactly a business is. With a laptop and a secure Internet connection it is now possible to create an online business with very little outlay in terms of financial or human resources.

The Internet has allowed the creation of new needs. Businesses such as Twitter, Groupon and LinkedIn have only been in operation for a few years, yet their influence is spreading. At the time of writing two of the most successful companies in the world are Google and Facebook. Both businesses respond to and satisfy customer needs.

Senior Business Studies   ISBN 9780170215732

What do we mean by small and medium-sized businesses?

It would be accurate to say that New Zealand is a small business nation. Small to medium-sized enterprises (SME) employing fewer than 19 people make up more the 91% of all firms. Most of New Zealand's SMEs contribute to the property or businesses services sector. This is also known as the tertiary sector.

Between 2000 and 2005, 85% of new businesses (also known as start-ups) had no employees. In total SME's produce over a third of the country's entire national output.

Number of enterprises by industry at February 2010

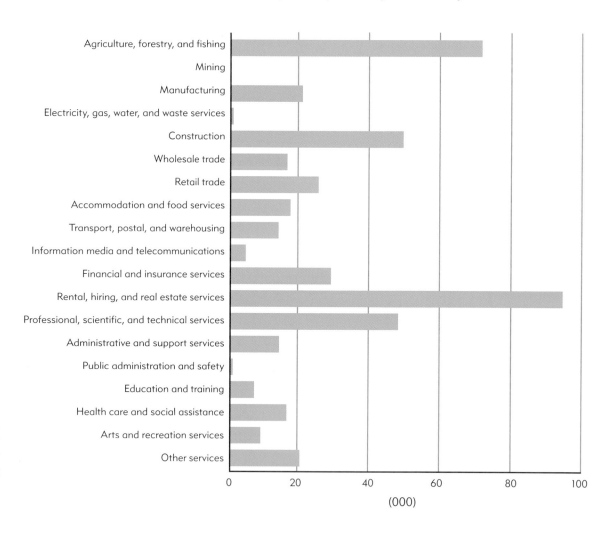

Senior Business Studies   ISBN 9780170215732

In 2010, 43,700 new business start-ups were registered or created, with 55,000 start-ups ceasing operations or going out of business. These figures demonstrate the well-known fact that we are very good at creating new business start-ups in New Zealand but keeping them going – or what business writers call making them 'sustainable' (see pages 40-43) – proves more challenging. Our economic future depends on the constant creation of new businesses that are sustainable.

Number of employees	Number of businesses		Total employees	
	2010	2005	2010	2005
0	323,935	293,237	0	0
1-5	97,888	96,588	225,930	223,510
6-9	19,571	19,873	141,040	143,710
10-19	15,980	16,148	213,710	215,960
20-49	8,420	8,712	249,570	258,210
50-99	2,489	2,487	170,670	170,470
100+	2,063	1,972	888,980	842,830

ACTIVITY

Review

- What do the results from the tables above indicate?

- You are thinking of setting up a business offering real estate advice to prospective homeowners under 30. Using the bar chart on page 8, what significant issues are you going to face in attracting customers?

Research

- What has happened to Bebo and MySpace?

- Using an Internet search engine, find the top ten most entrepreneurial countries in the world. New Zealand regularly features in the top ten. Can you think of any reasons why this should be the case?

ISBN 9780170215732

Why do we need business activity?

We tend to take businesses for granted, as if they have always been here. Modern economies need businesses to produce the goods and services that we need and want.

Definition

Needs are goods and services that are essential to sustain life. They include food, clothing, fuel for heating and transport, housing or the ability to communicate.

Wants are goods and services that add value to the lives of consumers but are not essential to sustain life. As consumers we can choose whether or not to purchase certain goods and services as wants, if we can afford them. Some wants remain elusive.

In introductory economics, students learn that resources are scarce, wants are unlimited, and that as individuals we have limited means (time, money and skills). This combination of unlimited wants and limited needs is known as the basic economic problem, and all consumers, businesses and governments experience it.

One solution to this problem is for individuals to specialise in the area in which they have the greatest skills, and then use those skills to exchange or purchase goods and services that they cannot produce themselves.

Successful businesses combine knowledge of production processes with minimising their costs to position themselves to satisfy wants and needs for consumers, and with a little creativity, innovation and foresight can even anticipate and satisfy new ones.

ACTIVITY

Discussion

- If there were no businesses, how much choice do you think consumers would have in purchasing goods and services?

- Do you think that consumers in New Zealand have too many choices? Refer back to the graph on page 8 to help you answer this question.

Future focus issues

There are two future focus issues that will be developed through this book: **enterprise** and **sustainability**. These will be looked at through all levels of the study of NCEA Business. Even though consumers will always have needs and wants, the global marketplace is such that these needs and wants can be satisfied by offshore businesses. Competition in all markets is considerable, and businesses cannot sit back and assume that consumers will continue to purchase their products indefinitely. New Zealand businesses of the future will need to be enterprising and sustainable.

For Level 2 students we need to add that businesses should also try to act in a manner that befits good **corporate citizenship** and **social responsibility**. We shall look at these big ideas in Unit 7.

A cultural snapshot of New Zealand: the impact on business activity

The 2011 census (cancelled due to the earthquake in Christchurch) would have provided the latest information about the cultural make-up or composition of New Zealand. Instead we can use the link to official statistics at www.stats.govt.nz. This website will become an important resource as we continue to examine trends in business activity.

As at June 2011, New Zealand's population consisted of 4.4m people, comprising:

- 68% who identified themselves as European.

- 15% who identified themselves as Māori.

- 10% who identified themselves as Asian.

- 7% who identified themselves as Pacific.

These statistics are evidence that New Zealand is a multicultural society, therefore our business communities or stakeholders (see pages 27-32) will also be multicultural.

Students at both Level 1 and 2 will need to identify and explain how New Zealand's cultural composition influences our business organisations and their operations. This important theme will be considered at every opportunity in the study of small and large businesses.

> Business education needs to equip students with the skills required for our future society. They should include emphasis on information technology, new forms of work, a multicultural and globalised society, and business and environmental issues. The rate of change is great. Students will need to reflect on changes in work patterns and philosophies, the growing cultural mix in our society, our increasing focus on Asian markets and environmental and technological changes.
>
> (Adapted, *Teaching and Learning Guidelines for Business Education*, November 2010)

ISBN 9780170215732

Senior Business Studies

Māori concepts

Students are required to show an understanding of Māori concepts and Asian cultural norms in business etiquette (see below) in their learning.

For Level 1 (2011) the key concept is **kaitiakitanga**. This concept features prominently in the extended case study on Kaikoura WhaleWatch (see pages 189-192).

For Level 2 (2011) there are five concepts to be investigated:

- **Tikanga**
- **Pūtake**
- **Tūranga**
- **Kaitiakitanga**
- **Rangatiratanga**

Teachers and students are recommended to check the guidelines at the beginning of the academic year for updates to this list of concepts.

Asian cultural norms

It would be unwise for any person wishing to work with Asian businesses either in New Zealand or overseas markets to ignore the cultural protocols or customary practices that are part of the Asian cultural value system.

These include but are not limited to:

- Do not embarrass an Asian manager or worker or put them in a position where they could 'lose face'.

- The importance of giving and receiving business cards when making a contact, even if it is just for a few minutes.

- When giving and receiving business cards with an Asian businessperson, it is important to offer a card with two hands rather than with one as is traditional in western cultures.

- Chinese business-people are superstitious about numbers. For instance $8.88 is considered a lucky price whereas $4.44 is considered very unlucky, in fact any price with a '4' in it is considered unlucky.

We will see examples of potential cultural confusion in the unit on communication (see pages 146-152). Misunderstandings can be created when we fail to observe the cultural values of a particular country.

Senior Business Studies   ISBN 9780170215732

Big idea 1: Risk-taking, innovation and the importance of creativity in business enterprise

At the end of this unit you will be able to:

- Define enterprise and give examples of enterprising behaviour.
- Identify the difference between invention and innovation.
- Explain risk-taking in a business context.
- Explain how creativity is important to businesses in New Zealand.

Definition

An **enterprise** is an activity or project a business or individual undertakes which is daring and courageous but with purposeful endeavour.

An entrepreneur (who is enterprising) uses their energy and initiative to act as a catalyst for change. They impact on the lives of stakeholders. A stakeholder is defined as any individual or group who is interested or directly affected by the activities of a business.

In some countries the term **social entrepreneur** is used to indicate that the purpose of the enterprise is to create positive benefits for stakeholders as a whole. Sir Ray Avery (New Zealander of the Year 2010), who has devoted much of his energy to creating life-enhancing medicines, is a good example of a social entrepreneur.

A key theme of the course you are studying is that young entrepreneurs should be socially responsible and create businesses that not only benefit the immediate stakeholders, but also the wider community where possible. This is not always easy to achieve.

Senior Business Studies   ISBN 9780170215732

New Zealand entrepreneurs

Many business students will be familiar with Stephen Tindall and Sam Morgan, who have become very well-known through their enterprising efforts. They have also managed to contribute hugely to the wider New Zealand community through charitable donations and providing finance for new enterprising ideas.

As we noted in the previous unit, New Zealand consistently appears in the list of the top ten most entrepreneurial countries in the developed world. Local and international surveys have regularly report that Māori are the third most entrepreneurial in the world. We have a rich history of successful (and some not so!) entrepreneurs and their enterprises.

Review

- Using examples from both New Zealand and the rest of the world, draw up a list of qualities that you think an entrepreneur should have.

- Now compare your list of qualities with a student sitting next to you. What do you notice?

- What would be the implication for New Zealand business and consumers if all entrepreneurs were identical in their thinking and personal qualities?

Discussion

- Given the personality types of entrepreneurs such as Sir Richard Branson, why do you think that some future entrepreneurs have found aspects of their education challenging?

Research

- Find out why Hell Pizza, Huffer t-shirts, Binary Star, Ice Breaker or Dawn Raid Entertainment are considered to be examples of New Zealand businesses that have taken considerable risks, and demonstrated enterprising attributes despite financial difficulties.

- Use Wikipedia to help you find out the biographies of some famous entrepreneurs like Sir Richard Branson and Sir Ray Avery.

ISBN 9780170215732

Enterprise and the need to take risks in business

'The difference between a successful person and a failure is not that one
has better abilities or ideas but the courage that one has to bet on one's
ideas to take a calculated risk – and to act.'

(Andre Malraux, 1901–76, French historian)

What is a risk?

Before looking at the reasons for starting a business, we need to consider a
very important element in business activity: Starting a business is risky. Read
the following account of a high school examination.

500 students were packed into an examination room, about to sit a very
important test. The top 50 students would receive scholarships (free places at a
famous university), and the top five students would receive a cash prize as well.
They sat nervously as the minutes ticked by, and at 9 am were told to begin.

The pressure was intense. Successful futures depended on doing well
here. Nervous and frightened students began the examination and turned
over the question paper. They had been told before the exam that there
would be four questions to answer. Instead there was only one on the paper
– a single question that could decide their future.

Nearly every student began writing furiously page after page of examples
and diagrams (well, wouldn't you?). The sound of pencils on paper was nearly
deafening in the silence. Long essay-type answers quickly began to appear.

On one student's desk, however, it was a different story.
This student looked at the question and then around the
room at everyone else writing, then picked up a pencil and
wrote only two words before putting their pencil down. The
student then got up from their seat and walked out, much to
the amazement of the 499 others, who must have thought the
student was crazy!

However, this individual received the top mark and a
scholarship. The two word answer has become legendary.

ISBN 9780170215732

Senior Business Studies

ACTIVITY

Discussion

- What two words did the student write?

- Write down and discuss three qualities a risk-taker must possess.

Research

- Find your own definition of risk.

- When it was first released in 2010, the Apple iPad was considered a risk. Why?

In addition to perseverance and determination, another key requirement of an entrepreneur is to take and manage risk.

Consider the example of enterprising behaviour and risk-taking from Auckland given below.

CASE STUDY

Sad Scenes at Outside Screening

Aucklanders are ignoring the open-air cinema at the viaduct harbour.

Watching movies in the fresh air is a popular summer activity but the Viaduct's new cinema is not proving to be successful.

Open Air Cinema project director Urs Bauer is surprised by the low turn-out to his new venture. Most movie screenings have attracted only a couple of hundred people each night, leaving empty seats out of a total of 2000. Business is looking grim.

Mr Bauer says that most people do not 'seem to get it.' They do not understand the reason to see the movie outside and often ask if they can take their cars into the venue. It is not a drive-in.

'I thought that potential consumers would be more willing to try,' said Mr Bauer.

Poor weather has not helped ticket sales and also Mr Bauer has been unable to generate funds for advertising on radio and TV. He has relied on word-of mouth promotion.

Despite disappointing turnouts, Mr Bauer is optimistic his enterprise will be sustainable.

Discussion

- Describe the risk that Mr Bauer and the Open Air Cinema have taken.

- Why do you think that 'most people do not seem to get it'?

- Explain whether you think using word of mouth promotion is an appropriate way to advertise a new enterprise such as the Open Air Cinema.

- How have external factors (outside Mr Bauer's control) impacted on Open Air Cinema?

- What is meant by the term 'sustainable business'?

- What advice would you give to Mr Bauer to make his business more sustainable? Explain your answer.

Thinking

The movie industry is a good example of where businesses regularly have to take risks. They can spend millions of dollars on hiring the best talent in front of and behind the camera and have great subject matter. However, this is no guarantee of success. *Star Wars* was offered by creator George Lucas to every major Hollywood studio in 1974 but they all turned him down. The film went on to become one of the most successful series of films in box office history and has earned over $US2b.

- Why do you think that every major film studio apart from one turned down the chance to make *Star Wars*?

- Why do you think that the movie business is considered risky compared to the food and beverage industry? Explain your answer.

Invention and innovation

The following example illustrates the difference between the two terms.

CASE STUDY

Martin Jet Pack lifts off

Glenn Martin of Christchurch created an international sensation when he exhibited his new invention – the Martin Jet Pack – at America's biggest consumer show EEA Airventure in Oshkosh, Wisconsin, in July 2008.

Glenn claims that his real-life jet pack will repay a near $1 million investment 20 times as he lines up customers around the world.

The Jet Pack was developed over 27 years and will reinforce New Zealand's reputation as a high-tech country.

Martin has had interest from a wide range of organisations around the world such as search and rescue, police and the military.

December 2008

ACTIVITY

Discussion

- Given this information do you consider that the Martin Jet Pack is a successful example of innovation?

- The photograph to the right is an example of Kiwi ingenuity after the Christchurch earthquake of 22 February 2011. Is it an example of invention or innovation?

ISBN 9780170215732

Senior Business Studies

ACTIVITY

Research

- Find out what happened to the founders of MITS (Micro Instrument Telemetry Systems) Ed Roberts and Forrest Mims, who are credited with developing the first commercially successful home computer, the Altair 8800 (at right).

- Why do you think that you may not have heard of Ed Roberts, as an innovator but you probably would have heard of one of the Mr Roberts most famous employees, William H. Gates?

Intellectual Property Rights (IPR)

It is very important that when creating a new invention – even if you think that the new product may have limited commercial appeal – that the inventor secures a **patent** to protect the **intellectual property right** to their idea.

Definition

Depending on the country they are issued in, a **patent** can give the inventor or firm the exclusive right to produce a product for up to 20 years. Check out www.iponz.govt.nz for further information.

It can be argued that patents protect intellectual property rights and the investment, which many small and large firms undertake when researching, developing and thus bringing to market new products.

In our earlier example regarding the Martin Jet Pack, the patent would protect the initial investment of $1 million if the new product went into production. This would then encourage other entrepreneurs to invest or develop new product ideas.

Some writers feel that patents protecting intellectual property rights can have significant benefits to both producers and consumers. The creation of an anti-malaria vaccine, for example, would be an enormous step forward in improving the lives of millions of people in the sub-Saharan African belt where malaria is most prevalent. Large pharmaceutical firms might be persuaded to finance the enormous sums of capital required to find such an elusive vaccine if there was a guarantee that, if successful, they would have exclusive rights over production to allow them the recoup these substantial costs.

Intellectual property rights

A Paeroa businessman has taken on a multi-national company in an intellectual property rights dispute over the phrase 'World Famous in New Zealand.'

Tony Coombe has objected to Coca-Cola Amatil's attempt to trademark the saying.

The dispute played out yesterday an Intellectual Property Office hearing in Auckland.

Coca-Cola has used the slogan to promote its L&P soft drink, which has its spiritual home in the Hauraki Plains town Paeroa, since 1993 – though the company applied for the trademark only in 2004.

But Mr Coombe owns a non-trading company named World Famous in New Zealand and said he believed the phrase 'Kiwi-ism', belonged to all New Zealanders. Coca-Cola disagreed, saying the words were clearly connected to its product and the trademark application should proceed.

Mr Coombe previously owned and ran the L&P Cafe in Paeroa with his business partner John Tregidga. After using the L&P name for six years, Coca-Cola forced the cafe and associated companies to change their titles.

The partners renamed the companies with their own initials (J&T), and Mr Coombe sold out in 2003 but still believes the use of the 'World Famous' phrase should be unrestricted.

Coca-Cola said that its advertising agency invented the slogan in 1993. A commissioner's decision expected in six to eight weeks.

An excellent film on the dangers of not securing clear IPR's over a new service is *The Social Network*, a film of the story of the famous legal act brought by the Vinklevoss twins and Eduardo Saverin against Mark Zuckerberg over the rights to the creation of Facebook. At time of writing this textbook the legal battle was continuing.

Review

- Why do you think that it is important to secure an intellectual property right through use of a patent?

- Explain one cost of not obtaining legal protection.

- What was the outcome of the case study above?

Factors that can lead to greater innovation

There is an excellent YouTube clip by Steven Johnson called 'Where do good ideas come from?' that neatly explains the origin of creative ideas and how this can lead to innovation. To summarise the main points of the clip:

- **Creative ideas rarely come to mind immediately** (what Johnson calls the 'eureka' moment). Instead innovation generally takes time (the 'slow hunch'). From the author's own experience of running the Young Enterprise scheme, one of the most difficult tasks is asking groups to come up with that great creative idea!

- **Creativity needs the 'right space'.** Interestingly, coffee houses in the early eighteenth century were where 'relaxed' discussions about new ways of thinking developed. (One is tempted to argue that school classrooms may not be an ideal environment to encourage creative discussions!)

- **Creativity needs collaboration.** In many cases, a creative idea needs nurturing by sharing the idea around a group of fellow students. Johnson argues that ideas need to 'collide'. With the availability of the Internet and social media, there are now many different ways to share and collaborate with other stakeholders.

Creativity and innovation

Many creative ideas have come from businesses *listening* to their customers, or by trying to *anticipate* future market trends. Creativity and innovation can come from analysing current and future trends and trying to come up with an idea that satisfies these as-yet unknown needs.

It is a not so well-known fact that many of the most popular items on the 105 menu, like the Big Mac and McChicken, were created not by the company but from suggestions by customers.

In recent times the Apple iPad was launched, despite many computer stakeholders who questioned the need for 'another kind of computing device' when many consumers already had desktop or laptop computers and smartphones. Given the enormous success of tablet computers launched by rival companies such as Sony, Samsung and Google it would appear that Apple's *anticipation* of future consumer needs and wants was correct.

ISBN 9780170215732

Senior Business Studies

Discussion

- What have you learned about the factors that can lead to innovation?

- How could you use some of the ideas highlighted in this chapter to help young New Zealanders be more successful innovators? (You may wish to look at some successful New Zealand entrepreneurs such as Sam Morgan to help you.)

- How important do you think technology, especially social media, has been and is going to be in the creation and development of new ideas?

- What has your research about the experiences of Bebo and MySpace told you about some of the problems of creating a new enterprise in an era of rapidly changing technology and consumer needs?

Research

- Google the following products:

    – Solar powered or clockwork radio.

    – The XO laptop.

    – The Q-Drum.

    Discuss in small groups why these products are considered to be examples of life-saving innovation.

The importance of aims and objectives

At the end of this unit you will be able to:

- Outline the importance of business aims and objectives.

In the next few units we are going to look at a number of topics that are common to all businesses and should be read by both Level 1 and 2 students.

Definition

A **business objective** is a statement (usually but not always in the form of a mission statement) which indicates a specific outcome(s) which a business wishes to achieve. An objective is often set in financial terms. This means that the objective can be expressed as a financial or monetary outcome. These could include:

- A target level of sales or profit for a financial year

- The level of growth in sales and profit over a financial period

- An increase in the value of the business to ensure survival.

A **business aim** is a general statement (usually but not always in the form of a vision statement) which indicates a longer term view/target of where a business sees itself moving to in the future. Businesses use an aim or vision to help guide senior management make their decisions. An aim has been referred to as a 'strategic declaration' to help guide stakeholders as to how a business will change and improve. It can also be used to motivate employees.

Senior Business Studies   ISBN 9780170215732

Definition

Profit: Total sales or revenue of the business less the total costs.

The importance of the profit motive to enterprise

We can state with certainty that the profit objective is considered to be the single most important reason for setting up a business. If an individual has decided to combine human and non-human resources in an enterprise and take a risk, then this profit is seen as the reward for success.

Consider that when one decides to begin a business there are significant **opportunity costs** involved, such as the loss of income that could be obtained from taking a full-time job instead of setting up their business, or the time given up at weekends to try and make the business economically sustainable and so on.

These opportunity costs may be significant, and therefore without the profit motive many individuals would not be willing to take the risk.

Evidence from New Zealand case studies suggests that some small businesses try to reach only a certain size and level of profitability because the opportunity costs of time and stress may impact on the quality of their lifestyle. When a business decides to do this, the business is said to be **profit satisficing**.

However, there are other aims and objectives we can explore:

* The need to be economically and ecologically sustainable within the community in the short run given the high rate of business failure within New Zealand (see Unit 6).

* The objective to be a good and responsible corporate citizen within the local and regional community (see Unit 7).

* The need for additional growth to become more sustainable in the long run.

* Given increasing competition in most markets, businesses may focus on cost minimisation to try and offer its customers the lowest prices. There are also other ethical objectives that a firm may wish to consider (see Unit 7).

* A business may have a key objective to be able to take advantage of new global trends in business activity, and become an export-driven business to Asia, South America or Europe (see Unit 27).

External environment and objectives/aims

The global economy is currently facing a number of challenges. It would be appropriate to say that, given the uncertain economic outlook, many small firms are struggling. When businesses set aims and objectives, they will have to take into account their **external environment** (see Unit 5).

Senior Business Studies   ISBN 9780170215732

Mission statements

A mission statement is a way of succinctly describing the reason for the existence of the business. They can help to clarify in the minds of stakeholders the purpose of the business, and to attract and retain customers, suppliers and investors. Some specific examples of mission statements may help to clarify this point:

'Connecting people has always been and continues to be our reason for business.' Nokia

Some writers have argued that mission statements are either too vague, inaccurate or unrealistic and can confuse stakeholders.

'To organise the world's information and make it more accessible and useful.' Google

Vision statements

A vision statement can be defined as a 'strategic declaration' of where the business sees itself moving towards in the future.

'Our vision is to become the world's leading company for automotive products and services.' Ford Motor Company

'Our vision is to be the world's premier food company, offering nutritious superior tasting foods to people everywhere.' Heinz

ACTIVITY

Research

- Find five mission statements from businesses that you are interested in.

- Research the mission statements of a Māori-owned and managed business to see how the concept of putake and kaitiakitanga can be applied.

- Now find three mission statements for three businesses in the same industry. Are they the same or different?

Thinking

- Why would you expect them to be different? Explain your answer.

Senior Business Studies   ISBN 9780170215732

Discussion

- Why do you that some small business owners may wish only to profit satisfice?

- Do you think that some vision statements are deliberately vague or imprecise? Why do you think this is the case?

- Consider the following mission statement of Philip Morris International, the producers of the Marlboro cigarette (the most popular brand in the world). Do you think this is an appropriate mission statement? Explain your answer.

> 'Our goal is to be the most responsible, effective and respected developer, manufacturer and marketer of consumer products intend for adults. Our core business is manufacturing and marketing the best quality tobacco to adults who use them.'

Stakeholders

At the end of this unit you will be able to:

- Identify the stakeholders of a business.

- Define what a stakeholder is and why they may have a direct or indirect effect on a business.

- Explain the reasons why stakeholders may disagree leading to stakeholder conflict.

Definition

A **stakeholder** in a business is any individual or group who is interested or directly affected by the activities of a business.

We are all stakeholders in one way or another. **Mahi ngatahi** is Māori for working together, and this points to the way shareholders are required to respect each others differences. The voice of every shareholder carries an equal weight when it comes to making decisions in business.

Stakeholders can be classified as either **internal** or **external**. Internal stakeholders include:

- Employees of the business.

- Shareholders, partners or owners.

- Senior managers who may carry out the mission or vision of the business.

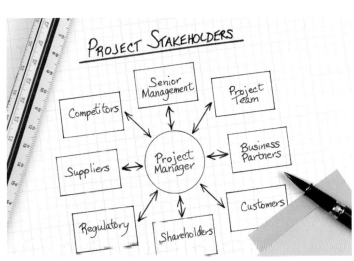

Senior Business Studies   ISBN 9780170215732

External stakeholders include:

- Suppliers to the business.
- Customers in both local and export markets.
- Pressure groups such as environmental protection groups, trade unions and employer associations who will aim to raise awareness of issues affecting their members collectively.
- Competitors who have an interest in any new idea or product that a business offers to the marketplace.
- The local community or iwi in which the business is located (important for small New Zealand firms).
- Regional and central government.
- Fiinancial instutions or lenders.

Consider the following stakeholders and their particular area of interest.

Stakeholder	Interest in the company
Owners/Shareholders/ Potential investors	Profit, mission statement, efficiency levels and current level of performance.
Government	Taxation (GST) compliance with occupational health and safety (OSH) (see Unit 5).
Senior managers	Financial performance, exercising control and making changes where necessary. Monitoring customer feedback. Profit and sales targets and setting new budgets if required.
Employees	Pay, working conditions, job security issues.
Customers	Value for money from purchasing goods and services of the business. Product quality and reliability. Ethical behaviour of the firm (see Unit 7) and corporate social responsibility.
Creditors	Cashflow and other financial issues of the business.
Local community	Social responsibility. The triple bottom line (see Unit 6).

Customers

IRD: Inland Revenue Department

A small bakery
Employing less than 20

Suppliers

Council

Local businesses as customers and competitors

Local business/employer associations
eg. Chamber of Commerce

Trade unions

IRD: Inland Revenue Department

A large manufacturing (secondary) business
Employing 240

Suppliers of primary resources

Supply chain retail

Central government

Overseas firms

Local government

Let us now put this knowledge to good use in the following case study, which illustrates how stakeholders may not always be in agreement.

CASE STUDY >>>

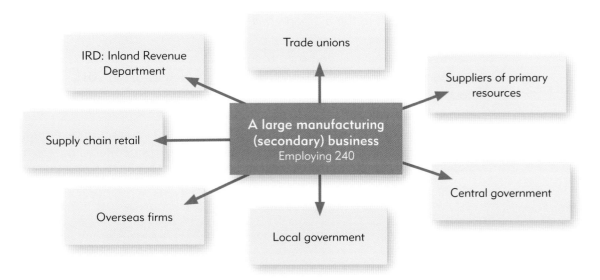

RWC economic scoreboard

COST $1,200m
Total spending identified in a Herald survey of tournament organisers, local authorities, government departments, public bodies, transport hubs and key sponsors.

INCOME $700m
Government estimate of direct economic returns.
BUT economist Tim Hazledine estimates "actual money-in-the-pocket benefits" will be $150 million

$500m Rugby World Cup deficit

New Zealand will spend more than $1.2 billion on investments backing the Rugby World Cup – but the tournament will make only $700 million in direct economic and business returns.

A Herald survey asked RWC organisers, local authorities, government departments, public bodies, transport hubs and sponsors what they had prepared for the World Cup and how much they would spend.

ISBN 9780170215732

Senior Business Studies

'The important thing is to understand the scale of this thing from New Zealand's point of view,' said Rugby World Cup Minister Murray McCully. 'It's way bigger than anything we've ever done before.'

Mr McCully said the World Cup would have lasting economic value for New Zealand, but probably more important was the country building its brand on the international stage.

'We convince more tourists to come here, we convince more businesses to do business here with New Zealand companies and enter partnerships with them,' he said.

Mr McCully said there was real value in an event such as the cup. 'We'll get about $700 million or so of income as a country from people coming to visit, and we also will be investing in assets that will provide a return for many years.'

But University of Auckland economics professor Tim Hazledine has said that the benefit to the economy will be much less than $700 million.

The tournament will be run at a loss, two-thirds – $26 million – will be covered by taxpayers, and the NZ Rugby Union will pay for the rest.

Martin Snedden, chief executive of Rugby New Zealand 2011, the tournament organisers, said there were many intangible benefits in having the cup in New Zealand.

'It's not easy to measure in hard dollar terms but you can understand, if you are aware of these events, the really extensive worldwide media coverage and television coverage it gets and just how much opportunity it has on the world stage – it goes to so many different countries.'

April 2011

ACTIVITY

Review

- Identify the stakeholders present using a mind map similar to the one on the prevous page.
- Identify any stakeholder conflicts before the tournament started.

Research

- Find out the final profit and loss figure to determine whether or not the 2011 Rugby World Cup was a success for New Zealand businesses.
- Explain whether any conflicts identified in your answer in your Review questions above were resolved after the tournament concluded.

Thinking

- What are some of the difficulties in trying to hear and please 'all voices' when a decision needs to be made?
- Do you think that the 2011 Rugby World Cup (involving 20 different countries) generated 'global opportunities' for small and large New Zealand businesses?
- What evidence or data would you need in order to support your answer?

Senior Business Studies   ISBN 9780170215732

Stakeholder conflict

It would be difficult (perhaps impossible) for any business or major sporting event to try and satisfy all the needs, wants and interests of every stakeholder. Some stakeholder disagreement or conflict is inevitable.

Read the following case study and answer the questions below. This example reflects the stakeholder conflict that exists within the mobile telecommunication industry in New Zealand. As a stakeholder in the mobile phone business yourself, you will probably have your own views on whether or not the changes below will have any real effect on your decision as to which provider you subscribe to.

CASE STUDY

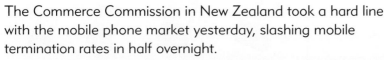

Rate cut aims to dial up competition

The Commerce Commission in New Zealand took a hard line with the mobile phone market yesterday, slashing mobile termination rates in half overnight.

In a long anticipated but expected decision, the regulator cut calling rates from 14 c to 7.8 c per minute and scheduled further cuts over the next three years.

By April 2012, the fees will be under 4 c and drop as low as 3.5 c by 2014.

SMS (texting) rates were cut from 9.5 c to 0.06 c per message.

Termination rates or (MTRs) are the fees telecommunication companies charge one another for a call or text message originating from a rival network. So if a Telecom customer calls a Vodafone mobile, Vodafone charges Telecom the fee.

It also applies when a call is made from a fixed-line such as a home phone to a mobile phone or if a text is sent to a rival network.

The sharp reduction in rates is aimed to stimulate competition within the industry.

'These changes are intended to address significant competition problems in the wholesale mobile market which have resulted in high retail prices – particularly for prepay customers – a low number of mobile calls and high rates of people switching networks, compared to other countries,' said Telecommunications Commissioner Ross Patterson.

Vodafone slammed the cuts as extreme. A spokesperson for Vodafone, Hayden Glass, said it was likely the company would ask the Commerce Commission for a review of the decision.

Mobile phone analyst Guy Hallwright said the Commerce Commission's decision could see Vodafone's profits fall by tens of millions of dollars and also

ISBN 9780170215732

reduce new investment in mobile networks needed to improve customer service.

Telecom the other major mobile network provider had already anticipated the reduction rates in its forecasts and the company seemed to take yesterday's decision in a positive way.

2degrees a new entrant in the New Zealand mobile market, on the other hand, was jubilant at news of the cuts. 'It's a great day for New Zealand mobile consumers,' said chief executive Eric Hertz.

Both Vodafone and Telecom indicated that they will not be lowering prices as a direct result of the rate reduction.

May 2011

Going down

The effect of the Commerce Commission's ruling on MTRs:

- 2010: 14 c (per minute)
- 2011: 7.48 c
- 1 October: 5.88 c
- 1 April 2012: 3.97 c
- 1 April 2013: 3.72 c
- 1 April 2014: 3.56 c

Senior Business Studies   ISBN 9780170215732

ACTIVITY

Small group exercise (Level 1)

- Use the case study above to define termination rates.
- Identify the key stakeholders for Vodafone.
- Explain the impact of the Commerce Commissions decision on your choice of mobile phone provider.

Small group exercise (Level 2)

- Describe two stakeholder conflicts indicated that could impact on Vodafone.
- Explain why the Commerce Commission decided to force mobile phone companies to reduce termination rates to customers.
- Vodafone and Telecom have said that they will not cut their rates to customers. Describe how other stakeholders such as 2degrees or other mobile network providers may react.

The external environment

5

At the end of this unit you will be able to:

- Identify legal, economic and environmental constraints on business.
- Describe competition in the local business environment.

When we consider the external environment we are looking at a range of factors or influences outside the control of the business, which may either restrict or enhance that businesses ability to meet its objectives.

External factors can lead to both opportunities and threats for the business concerned.

NCEA Level 1: External influences include Legal, Economic and Environmental.

NCEA Level 2: External influences include Political, Social, Technological and Ethical.

Factors of the external environment

One useful way to remember all seven factors of the external environment is to use the abbreviation STEEPLE.

 Social

Society changes over time. Every five years the New Zealand government conducts a census to find out what these changes might be. Consumer tastes and preferences are just one small part. Family size, working patterns and attitudes towards a whole range of social issues affecting small and large businesses need to be considered.

Senior Business Studies   ISBN 9780170215732

Technological

The Internet and social networking sites such as Facebook and Twitter have created many significant opportunities for businesses to reach and communicate directly with their stakeholders. One could argue that if a business does not have a web presence of some kind it runs the risk of going out of business, as it is more likely that their competitors will use online technology to their advantage.

Moore's Law states that the rate of change of technological process is likely to dramatically increase. Businesses now have to look at how they produce goods and services or whether or not they should allow another business – perhaps outside New Zealand – to do it for them (see Units 18 and 27).

Technology has had a major impact on the way businesses carry out promotion and marketing, especially with the development of YouTube.

 Economic

There are numerous economic factors in the external environment, such as the number of firms in competition with the business start-up, consumer and business confidence for the future, or the value of the dollar and the rate of interest on money that firms may need to borrow to get the business going.

If the New Zealand economy is in a **recession** (defined by economists as two sequential economic quarters of falling output or spending) then the impact on consumer confidence will be considerable.

Economic factors can also be linked to other countries, which can create either opportunities or threats for businesses here in New Zealand. The rapid growth of the Chinese economy and emerging Asian markets in general are very good examples of economic factors affecting New Zealand's external environment.

 Environmental

Growing global awareness of the environmental impact of business by stakeholders has forced many companies to consider the size of their environmental or ecological footprint. Some company websites now include detailed references explaining how they are trying to be environmentally sustainable.

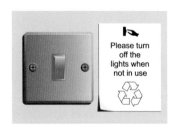

In Australia the introduction of the Carbon Tax generated significant debate and will bring considerable challenges for both small and large businesses to meet their commitment to ecological sustainability.

Senior Business Studies   ISBN 9780170215732

Political

The government will have an inevitable impact on business, whether directly through legislation such as the Consumer Guarantees or Fair Trading Acts, or indirectly through its management of the economy. We shall see in a later unit the impact of the introduction of the 90-day employment trial period on employee rights and responsibilities in businesses in New Zealand.

 Legal

This is linked to political factors (see above), and is the need for businesses to observe the legal requirements of setting up a business, paying corporation (profit) tax and GST to the IRD, and generally following the rules for activities such as advertising, health and safety (OSH) and other types of employment legislation. The requirement of the legal system in New Zealand to guarantee intellectual property rights for hopeful inventors and innovators was presented in Unit 2.

 Ethical

As we shall see in Unit 7, an increasing trend for small and large businesses is that they have to consider the growing stakeholder expectation that businesses need to be more ethical. The use of online social media has meant that business activities can be put 'under the microscope' more than ever before.

Students may wish to look at the case of the two New Zealand students who challenged GlaxoSmithKline about their claim that Ribena in Australia contained sufficient Vitamin C, or the controversy around the true price of an All Black rugby jersey. The example of the KFC Double Down Burger (in Unit 7) is another case where one could argue that the company was acting unethically by selling their bread-less chicken sandwich. Other real life examples of ethics in business include the selling of 'legal high' substances, a particularly controversial issue.

PEST in action

Now let us apply another version of the analysis of external factors in the environment to a small business example: PEST (Political, Economic, Social, Technological). Note that not all factors will apply to every business.

ISBN 9780170215732

CASE STUDY

How a world of downloads killed the Groove in Wellington

In the corner, a vinyl lover looks through the bargain bin. Over by the counter a mother with baby wanders towards the cassette tapes. A young man in a hoodie, headphones around his neck, flicks through electronic music section. Older customers look through the latest albums – and the old – in blues, techno, house, folk. The list of diverse customers goes on. Real Groovy is as busy as any shop in Cuba St, Wellington this weekday afternoon. However, the closing-down sale signs out the front may explain why.

Inside a backroom office, Mark Thomas, 37, is probably the biggest music lover in the place. He is thumbing through correspondence from his landlord.

On May 31, Real Groovy Wellington will shut its doors for the last time. The recession, big chains selling at cut prices, and the download revolution have all taken their toll on the independent store. This despite Real Groovy having set up their own online store.

It will be the end of an era for Wellington's music lovers, but the end of a dream for Mr. Thomas, the Whakatane-born, Waikato-bred owner of Real Groovy Wellington since 2008. Mr. Thomas managed the shop since it opened in 1999, and mortgaged his house to buy the business after its parent company went into receivership.

He hopes to open a smaller record store if he can. But right now he is focused on shutting down Real Groovy and keeping hold of his house, which he shares with his wife and three kids.

May 2011

From the case study we can note:

 Political factors

For this Real Groovy case study, the political factors will have, at best, a weak or indirect impact. Some stakeholders of Real Groovy may urge the government to create new assistance schemes to help small businesses struggling to deal with the effects of the slowdown in the economy. Of course if Real Groovy specifically were to receive financial support, other small businesses in Wellington may feel that they deserve the attention too. It would appear that the E, S and T factors are having a more direct influence on the success or failure of the business.

Senior Business Studies   ISBN 9780170215732

Economic factors

The recession, both in New Zealand and overseas, would have impacted on Real Groovy's sales. Secondly, competition from large retail chains such as The Warehouse, which would also have impacted on sales of records sold at Real Groovy.

 Social factors

The change in consumer habits which occur when society changes. In this case study it has occurred because consumers such as yourselves now enjoy their music by using digital media, and the prevalence of peer-to peer websites (made illegal from 1 September 2011).

It should be noted that there is a core group of consumers who still wish to listen to music on vinyl, who have created something called a niche market (see Unit 13).

 Technological factors

The software and hardware that allowed the downloading to take place. However, this has also allowed Real Groovy to set up its own website to allow customers to browse online.

We will now undertake a STEEPLE analysis on two large businesses in the same industry, to see how external factors can impact on decision-making.

Air New Zealand's Green Flight Makes History

It was a history-making flight but it looked all very ordinary – and that's just how Air New Zealand wanted it.

The airline yesterday completed the world's first commercial aviation test flight using biofuel to power one of its Boeing 747-400's Rolls-Royce engines. The biofuel is a 50:50 blend of jatropha and Jet A1 fuel.

The jatropha plant – which Air New Zealand sourced from Africa and India – produces seeds that contain inedible lipid oil, which is used to produce fuel.

Air New Zealand chief pilot Captain Dave Morgan told reporters and Air New Zealand staff by satellite phone that the flight was uneventful – and he couldn't have been more pleased.

Senior Business Studies   ISBN 9780170215732

Air New Zealand chief executive Rob Fyfe said the test flight showed the airline was at the forefront of making bio-fuel commercially viable. It was another step in the long-term goal to become the world's most environmentally sustainable airline.

Prime Minister John Key congratulated Air New Zealand on the successful test flight.

He added that it was a historic day and he was proud the airline was working with world leaders in their fields to develop more sustainable fuels.

The test flight was a joint initiative by Air New Zealand, Boeing and Rolls Royce.

December 2008

If you don't fit, buy two seats

It's only a matter of time before other airlines start demanding obese passengers pay for two seats, an aviation commentator says.

Peter Clark said the number of very large people boarding aircraft was increasing and people who struggle to get into one seat should pay the extra cost.

His comments follow reports that Air France-KLM planned to make overweight passengers pay for a second seat.

The airline denies it would make obese passengers pay more and says the only recent change is they will refund the cost of the second seat, if one is bought, if the economy cabin is not full.

The extra seat came with a 25% discount.

Mr Clark said airlines would soon have to start asking bigger passengers to pay for another seat or take a bigger one in premium economy or business class.

Safety issues were also involved with very large people in planes, such as moving quickly in an emergency or even putting a seat belt on.

'A large person can create problems if they impede the movement of other passengers or if they have to evacuate quickly … It's a confined space and if someone is impinging on the space of another passenger – who has paid a lot of money for it – then that's not fair.'

However, Mr Clark did concede that there would be human rights issues if airlines did ask fat passengers to pay more but safety should come first.

An Air New Zealand spokesperson commented that they expect passengers who know they require extra room to buy another seat to get the space they required. At the time of the flight, if there are spare seats, Air New Zealand always tries to accommodate passengers requiring extra room,' a spokeswoman said, 'whether this is people travelling with children or for medical or personal reasons'.

January 2010

ISBN 9780170215732

Senior Business Studies

ACTIVITY

Review

- Identify the external influence(s) affecting the businesses in the first article, and explain how these influences have impacted on decision-making.

- Carry out a STEEPLE analysis on the airline industry. Explain why airlines have to consider changes in the social and legal factors you identify.

Discussion

- Do you think that airlines are being ethical or fair by charging larger passengers more for extra space or a seat?

- Explain any one stakeholder conflict in this case study.

- Fully explain a solution to one of the conflicts identified above.

Research and Thinking

- Can you think of any recent government policies that have impacted on a small business?

- Carry out some research on the pizza industry in New Zealand, paying close attention to the introduction of both Domino's and Hell Pizza. Then undertake a STEEPLE analysis for Domino's and Hell Pizza.

- Are there any similarities or differences in your analysis?

- For Level 2 students: Do you think that Hell Pizza act ethically?

- Does your answer about what is considered to be 'ethical' depend on your age and point of view?

Big idea 2: Sustainability

At the end of this unit you will be able to:

- Define sustainability in terms of the 'triple bottom line'.
- Identify sustainable business practices (economic, environmental/ecological and social).
- Understand why sustainability in all its forms is important to New Zealand business.
- Understand the key factors that have lead to New Zealand small businesses not being sustainable.

One of the major themes or 'big ideas' of the business studies course is the issue of sustainability.

Definition

A **sustainable** business meets the needs of present stakeholders without compromising the ability of future generations of stakeholders to meet their own needs.

Sustainable development of a business can further be defined as a 'strategy that requires the integration of **economic growth**, **social equity**, and **environmental management**. Sustainable development aims to make global society not just better off, but better altogether.'

This definition is important as it emphasises the need for both small and large businesses to look beyond the **environmental or ecological impact**. In order to be truly sustainable, a business should also consider its **economic** influence through the selling of goods and services, and also try to develop **social equality** within the community in which the business operates.

ISBN 9780170215732

The New Zealand Business Council has referred to this as the 'the triple bottom line' and there are similarities to the Māori concept of tuhono or 'to join'. To see whether a business satisfies the needs of the triple bottom line of sustainable development, a business needs to ask itself three primary questions:

1 **Economic sustainability**: Does my product or service which I am offering benefit my company in financial (that is, monetary) terms?

2 **Environmental or ecological sustainability**: Does this product or service benefit or protect the natural systems that my company relies on?

3 **Social sustainability**: Does this product or service benefit the community and society where my company operates?

The importance of economic sustainability

As we saw in Unit 1, the number of business that have expired or ceased trading in 2010 exceeded the number that started up.

According to another survey from the New Zealand Herald, businesses with no employees are the most likely to fail, and figures suggest that 80% of new business start-ups fail or cease trading within the first two years. 75 % will fail within three years.

There is much that can be learnt from the lessons of unsuccessful entrepreneurs in the past.

The importance of ecological sustainability

The environmental component or ecological sustainability is probably the most familiar one to students. Ecological sustainability is achieved if the present generation of businesses ensures that the heath, diversity and productivity of the environment is monitored or even enhanced for the benefit of future generations. Sustainability in this sense most closely ties in with the Māori concept of Kaitiakitanga which we alluded to at the beginning of this unit. Please note ecological sustainability demands that the impact of environmental factors created by business should be included in the final prices charged by businesses for their goods and services. One could argue that this aspect of ecological sustainability could conflict with economic sustainability if a new business prices its products above that of the existing competition.

The importance of social sustainability

Since New Zealand is a nation of small businesses, sustainability is vital. Away from the big commercial centers of Auckland, Christchurch or Wellington, rural areas rely on sustainable businesses not only to provide employment but also to keep their communities thriving and socially sustainable.

Rural communities are particularly effective at encouraging young people to become the next generation of entrepreneurs, so that their community can be sustained and the cycle repeated.

Read the following case study and answer the questions on the next page.

ISBN 9780170215732

ANZ: Sustainability in action in New Zealand

ANZ Banking Group has been named the world's most sustainable bank in the 2010 Dow Jones Sustainability Index for the fourth consecutive year.

The annual DJSI review analyses the corporate, environmental and social performances of sustainability leaders from each industry on a global and regional level.

It assesses issues such as corporate governance, risk management, branding, and climate change awareness and labor practices.

ANZ New Zealand deputy chief executive Steven Fyfe said he is pleased ANZ New Zealand 'is making an important contribution to helping the ANZ Group stay at the top of the index, alongside some of the most respected and successful companies in the world.'

He said ANZ's corporate responsibility efforts concentrate on customer focus, helping communities grow, and creating a risk aware culture.

'An example is our Financial Wellbeing programme in New Zealand which was established to support personal customers facing financial difficulty as a result of the global financial crisis. Since August 2008 we have directly assisted more than 8,500 customers through this programme,' Fyfe said.

This year, ANZ partnered with Te Rūnanga o Ngāi Tahu, the governing body for Ngāi Tahu Whanui, to undertake the world's first indigenous people's financial knowledge survey.

'We're also proud of the active role our staff play in our communities. They have donated more than 15,000 volunteer hours – that's more than 2000 days – to community organisations, projects and charities this year.'

September 2010

ACTIVITY

Review

- Identify one economic, one social and one cultural sustainable business practice from the case study on ANZ. Explain why you think that ANZ invest time and resources in developing and following sustainable business practices.

- Outline the benefits to Ngāi Tahu Whanui of the financial knowledge survey.

- For Level 2 students: Fully explain whether or not you think that ANZ is acting as a 'good corporate citizen'.

Why is the rate of start-up business failure so high?

There are many reasons why businesses in New Zealand struggle, and not all of them are linked to insufficient finances. As we saw in a Unit 5, a number of contributing factors may be completely outside the control of the entrepreneur. (Refer to the previous example of the open-air cinema owner on page 16.)

Consumer tastes may simply change and move away from your product or service for reasons you cannot fully explain despite having carried out market research.

In their book *Small Business Survival* Glen Senior and Ian McBride note the following reasons why so many small businesses find it difficult to be economically sustainable:

- Lack of a support network.
- Poor management skills.
- A lack of business experience.
- A slowdown in the economy or industry that the firm operates in.
- Over-ambitious sales targets.
- Over-spending in fixed assets or capital.
- Poor collection of revenue from customers.
- The business has too much unsold stock.

The *New Zealand Herald Business Guide* added to this:

- Initial enthusiasm for the reason for the business starts to disappear.
- The bright innovative ideas start to dry up.
- Poor cashflow, planning and management.

ACTIVITY

Discussion

- Why do you think that new small businesses may be able to satisfy one aspect of sustainability but not the other two at the same time? A small business may be able to satisfy the environmental component, but not the social or economic?
- Discuss the role that lack of finance has played in explaining why small businesses fail to be economically sustainable.

Research

- Can you find any examples of New Zealand businesses both small and large that satisfy the triple bottom line? (Hint: Locally-owned companies such as Sealord and Sanford are useful places to start.)

ISBN 9780170215732

Senior Business Studies

Big idea 3: Corporate and social responsibility (CSR) and citizenship

At the end of this unit you will be able to:

- Define corporate social responsibility and citizenship.

- Explain what is meant by ethical behaviour.

- Explain ethical issues relating to business activities.

- Outline how and why business can contribute to the development and well being of society.

Before we begin our review of these large concepts, read the following case involving a well-known product that generated a number of 'column inches' in newspapers and broadcast media in May 2011.

CASE STUDY

The KFC Double Down Burger

Fast food junkies eager to get their hands on the new KFC Double Down burger will need to walk for around 80 minutes to burn off the burger's 604 calories, a nutritionist says.

The long-awaited bun-less burger will be available at KFC outlets around the country from 10 am tomorrow – and if the 'Bring the KFC Double Down Burger to New Zealand' Facebook page with its more than 2,000 members is anything to go by, there may be a long queue.

However nutritionists have condemned the Double Down's high calorie and fat count.

A single Original Recipe Double Down – which comprises two strips of

bacon, cheese and 'the Colonel's special sauce' encased in two chicken fillets – has 604 calories, 12.6 grams of carbohydrates, 57.6 g of protein and a total of 34.4 g of total fat, 11.9 g of which is saturated fat.

KFC general manager Brent Kitto acknowledged the Double Down is not for everyone, saying it is an 'occasional meal.' 'Contrary to all the attention and speculation though, the Double Down is actually lower in calories and fat than a number of other burgers already on the market,' he said. 'However, the Double Down breaks the mold. With two of everything, there's simply no room for the bun, just the best stuff – chicken, bacon, cheese and the Colonel's special sauce.'

Healthy Food Guide nutritionist Claire Turnbull said it would take 80 minutes of 'brisk walking' to burn off the calories from the Double Down. 'The first thing to say is that they're one of the highest calorie items on their menu ... and one of the highest fat items in a single serving,' she said. 'What you also have to remember is at KFC people are not going to just eat this on its own. They might order it with fries and a drink.'

While the calories in the burger are only slightly higher than the average meal, Ms Turnbull said people need to worry about the total amount and the types of food they are eating and the frequency they are eating. 'The reality is society has accepted this kind of food and people are consuming it more frequently than they need it.'

Ms Turnbull said while KFC might call it an 'occasional meal' many people will indulge in the Double Down more frequently than they should. 'I'm all about people having personal choice. In this country some fast food outlets have made some responsible choices and that is awesome. It lies down to individuals wanting to make that choice. I don't blame it on the fast food joints themselves.'

The Double Down will only be available for five weeks, costing $7.90 for just the burger and $10.90 for a combo.

(The burger was available in New Zealand stores for five weeks. One local newspaper estimated that 60,000 were sold during this time.)

May 2011

Review and Inquiry

- Define and explain the term corporate social responsibility.

- Explain why corporations would wish to be socially responsible.

- Explain why some businesses have set 'ethical objectives'.

- List examples from your own experiences of how a fast food business has been creative and innovative with a new product.

- Explain whether these new and creative products could be considered 'ethical'

ACTIVITY

ISBN 9780170215732

ISBN 9780170215732

ACTIVITY

Discussion

- Do you think that KFC are being socially responsible by releasing the Double Down Burger?

- Is the Double Down Burger an ethical product?

- Do you think that KFC have been innovative with the Double Down Burger?

- Has KFC anticipated a new trend in consumer needs and wants?

Use the Internet to find definitions of **citizenship**, **tikanga** and **ethical behaviour**.

Corporate social responsibility (CSR) and citizenship

Definition

Corporate social responsibility: 'The continuing commitment by business to behave ethically and contribute to economic development while improving the quality of life of the workforce and their families (whanau) as well as of the local community (iwi) at large.'

(Edward Russell-Walling, quoting the World Business Council, 2007)

'Businesses have no social responsibility other than to increase profits and refrain from deception and fraud. When businesses seek to maximise profits they always do what is good for society.'　　　(Milton Friedman)

Corporate social responsibility (CSR) and citizenship are strongly interconnected and have very similar definitions, so to avoid unnecessary confusion this guide will treat them the same. One could argue that if a business adopts a CSR approach, then it is being a good corporate citizen.

The reader may be surprised to discover that there is still considerable debate over whether or not firms need to be socially responsible, consider the quotation above from Milton Friedman. However, by looking at the World Business Council definition below it would appear that all firms should adopt a CSR approach, since firms who did not would be unpopular with their stakeholders.

ACTIVITY

Discussion

- What are the difficulties for a small or large business adopting a CSR approach?

- Why might some stakeholders (or interested groups) be critical or skeptical of a business adopting a CSR approach?

Thinking

- The discussion above would have illustrated that it is difficult to reach agreement as to what is considered to be truly ethical or socially responsible. If we add international comparisons into our thinking, then the picture can become confusing. Consider the table below of the brands in New Zealand, the UK and the US, that are perceived as behaving ethically.

  Are there any surprises in the table for New Zealand or the US?

  Can you add any other examples?

Rank	UK	US	NZ (ethical)	NZ (CSR)
1	The Co-op	Coca-Cola	Ecostore	ANZ
2	Body Shop	Kraft	Toyota	Telecom
3	Marks and Spencer	Proctor and Gamble	Meridian	The Warehouse
4	Traidcraft	Nike	Air NZ	ACC
5	Café Direct	Sony	Body Shop	NZ Post

Ethical objectives

If a business sets an ethical objective, it means that the business wishes to be regarded as morally correct and appropriate in the minds of its stakeholders.

Some examples will help clarify our understanding of what an ethical objective could look like. In each of the following cases the company is trying to 'do the right thing', and have an objective that is acceptable to all those with an interest in the organisation.

ISBN 9780170215732

Senior Business Studies

- A large New Zealand business operates in a country where the government imposes strict controls on working conditions and the use of child labour in manufacturing.

- A pharmaceutical company decides to price a new vaccine for the cure of a tropical disease in a poor country with a high incidence of that disease at an affordable price given local income levels.

- A tobacco or alcoholic drinks company avoids sponsoring any sporting or entertainment event where young consumers may be in the crowd.

Some companies give large sums of money back to communities in the form of philanthropic grants and donations. Many donations are not made public.

One UK entrepreneur re-invented the notion of business as one where 'profits can be earned by principles'. Young entrepreneurs in New Zealand could learn much by following her example.

CASE STUDY

Anita Roddick DBE
(1942–2007)

Dame Anita Roddick, outspoken founder of cosmetic giant The Body Shop and one of the world's most famous businesswomen, has died at the age of 64.

Launched in Brighton (UK) in 1976, The Body Shop sells health and beauty products sourced from natural ingredients or produced using ethical processes. Roddick's initial idea was to provide skin and hair care products in refillable containers. Her company quickly grew and became the late-twentieth century's poster-child for environmentally sustainable, socially responsible business.

Born Anita Lucia Perilli, Roddick said it was her Italian mother's frugality during World War Two that inspired her to campaign for environmental issues. 'We reused everything, we refilled everything and we recycled all we could. The foundation of The Body Shop's environmental activism was born out of ideas like these,' she wrote. The Body Shop's mission statement ('To dedicate our business to the pursuit of social and environmental change') reflects these values.

Roddick eventually became a multi-millionaire and saw her retail empire balloon to over 2000 outlets stores across 51 different markets. 'The Body Shop is not, and nor was ever, a one-woman-show,' she said, 'it's a global operation with thousands of people working towards common goals and sharing common values.' The Body Shop was sold to L'Oreal in 2006 for over NZ$1b.

September 2007

Senior Business Studies   ISBN 9780170215732

CASE STUDY

Facebook and technology: a force for good?

After the September earthquake in Christchurch last year, Sam Johnson started a 200-member Facebook page to co-ordinate students who wanted to help. Within a short time, the page catered to 2500 students cleaning up the liquefaction issues that resulted from that first quake.

Back then, Apple NZ contributed three iPhones to help them communicate; these were gratefully received and worked effectively in managing this earthquake.

I asked Sam why he set up the Student Volunteer Army: 'I saw a need and wanted to help. I wasn't personally affected at all. But there didn't seem to be any way to get large numbers of volunteers working with the existing agencies. There was no volunteer co-ordination, so I set it up, with key helpers.'

The team of six around Sam determined to keep the momentum after the first quake, with student-community engagement. This team comprised Sam plus Gina Scandrett, Chris Duncan, Jade Rutherford, Tom Young and Sam Gifford.

Continuing operations after the September quake proved fortuitous – when the second quake hit, earlier this year, Sam says everything 'was ten times the scale of the first.'

This group of six extended out to a core team of 12 who ran the February earthquake service, each heading a different department. 'In total we had around 75 staff volunteering in the different departments.'

Within a short time, the Student Volunteer Army had 7000 to 8000 students out on the streets, totting up 75,000 hours worked alongside Civil Defence, the authorities and relief agencies. The will of students to work at the backbreaking tasks awed people all around New Zealand, and the world.

April 2011

ISBN 9780170215732

Senior Business Studies

Thinking

- Why is it so difficult to accurately define what 'doing the right thing' is?

- Is 'doing the right thing' the same for teenagers as opposed to their parents or elders?

- Explain whether or not you think supermarkets should be allowed to stock and sell RTDs (Ready to Drink) or pre-mixed 'alcopops'.

Research

- Find out about the Stephen Tindall Foundation and Ronald McDonald House in New Zealand.

- Why do you think these organisations give so generously?

- What is philanthropy?

- How is the Stephen Tindall Foundation and Ronald McDonald House in New Zealand examples of philanthropic behaiour?

- Research the creation and development of The Body Shop. How was Anita Roddick's approach to running a business different to so many other cosmetic companies?

Inquiry

- Explain why you think that Facebook is often criticised as being unethical.

- Using information above, fully explain how using Facebook has lead to citizenship and ethical behaviour in New Zealand.

- Using this case study, or other examples from your own experience, explain how using technology may lead to social responsibility.

Business success

At the end of this unit you will be able to:

- Define different types of business success.

- Explain why measuring business success is difficult to accurately define for small and large businesses given the external environment.

We looked earlier at some of the reasons why many small businesses in New Zealand are not economically sustainable. To provide some balance to this point of view, however, we should remember that in many cases, both locally and globally, several businesses have been hugely successful.

Business success is a difficult term to accurately define. Success for one firm may be viewed as a failure for another. For example:

- If a new business start-up survives the first year of trading then it could be considered a success, even if it has not generated a profit – but it is sustainable.

- The Rugby World Cup may not generate a profit for New Zealand after the tournament ends, but there have been significant future benefits for many stakeholders.

- A very small profit for Restaurant Brands (owners of KFC in New Zealand) may be considered disappointing. But for 2degrees, a new entrant into a market already dominated by large existing businesses, this would be considered a superb achievement.

Consequently we have to be careful before we can judge business success.

Senior Business Studies   ISBN 9780170215732

There are a number of accepted ways that we can judge **business success**. Some of them are based on the view of various stakeholders:

- The business is viewed as creating innovative and ethical products.

- Being sustainable according to the triple bottom line.

- Being viewed as a responsible corporate citizen and with positive feedback from its internal and external stakeholders.

Other measures of business success are considered in financial terms:

- Increasing profits allowing higher dividends to owners and shareholders.

- Increasing sales and growing market share.

- The ability to enter and grow into new international markets.

CASE STUDY

Vodafone loses 26K customers in June quarter

Vodafone New Zealand, the country's biggest mobile phone operator, lost 26,000 customers in the June quarter as new entrant Two Degrees Mobile Ltd. ate into its market share.

Auckland-based Vodafone had 2.458 million customers as at June 30, down from 2.484 million three months earlier.

That is the lowest number of customers on Vodafone's books since June last year, when the company shed 35,000 customers.

However, it's not all bad news for Vodafone, with the percentage of pre-paid customers, which are traditionally lower profit-generating falling. Vodafone still has 67% of the pre-paid market.

Its proportion of pre-paid customers has been steadily declining for the past couple of years as mobile operators try to switch clients on to post-paid plans, which include more attractive broadband data services.

The news comes as 2degrees continues its push to win customers from Vodafone and Telecom having entered the market two years ago.

In March this year, 2degrees said it cornered about 11% of the nation's market with 580,000 customers.

Heavy investment costs of building a network means that 2 degrees posted a $76.8 million loss on revenue of $107.6 million in the 12 months ended December 31.

July 2011

ACTIVITY

Review

- How many customers did Vodafone lose from March to June 2011?

- Using material from the case study, why would Vodafone not be concerned that it is losing pre-paid customers to companies such as 2degrees?

- Vodafone still controls 67% of the mobile phone market. Explain whether or not they would feel threatened by 2degree's success?

- Given the information in the case, explain why it is difficult to measure business success based simply on one year's worth of financial data.

- What other information would you require to judge the success of both Vodafone and 2degrees?

Research

- 2degrees had 580,000 customers in June 2011. Identify from research two reasons why they have been successful despite making a loss of $76.8m.

Small business success

Despite falling market share, Vodafone are still in a very strong position in the mobile phone market and it will be some years before we can really judge the success of 2degrees. It is tempting to ask, 'How long can 2degrees continue to compete against Vodafone, given that they are currently making a loss?'

Judging small business success is even more difficult. We noted in Unit 2 that most small businesses in New Zealand do not survive their first two years of trading. Just being able to **breakeven** (when your total sales revenue exactly equals your total costs) may be considered a success.

ISBN 9780170215732

Senior Business Studies

53

One could also argue that the true measure of success is a business owner's ability to cope, or to reflect and learn from past mistakes. Success could be a demonstration of resilience, or turning a passion into a sustainable business idea.

Consider the contrasting experiences of Tasty Pot and Dawn Raid, and answer the questions that follow.

CASE STUDY

Success: Fresh approach cooking up a storm

Tasty Pot is a new Auckland-based company whose success is based on a simple premise: fresh vegetable gourmet meals that can be bought off supermarket shelves.

Since June 2010, the company has managed to get its products – meals that take four minutes to heat and are beautifully presented in clear plastic containers – into New World and Progressive supermarket chains and premium price food outlets such Nosh and Farro.

In November Tasty Pot competed against its rivals at the New Zealand Food Awards and won three prizes, including the Supreme Award. It was the cuisine equivalent of David beating Goliath as previous winners included Tegel, Tip Top, Watties, Sealord, Hubbard Foods and the New Zealand Dairy Board.

The company now produces more than 600 pots a day at its Penrose factory and has the capacity to triple output as demand grows.

'What we're good at is good, honest food,' says Andrew Vivian, who founded the company with his wife, Natalie, in April.

Tasty Pot's runaway success is built partly on growing public concern about diet and the need to eat healthier food. Of the six products, which will include different seasonal offerings, three are vegan recipes and three are gluten-free, the latter a growth market in the food sector.

It also packs its meals by hand adding a quality touch to its finished product, which has been fully appreciated by its customers.

'The nicest thing isn't the number of stores we're in, it's the feedback we're getting from consumers,' he says. 'That is the gauge of success … new recipes will be unveiled this year and are likely to include a meat dish. June is targeted as the point in which the operation will break even. Not bad for one year in business.'

February 2011

Senior Business Studies   ISBN 9780170215732

CASE STUDY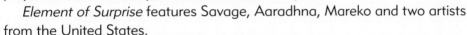

New sun shines on Dawn Raid label

With the release of a new album, *Element of Surprise*, Dawn Raid is back.

The work is founder Danny 'Brotha D' Leaosavaii's first album in years and the label's first project since it was saved from liquidation in July. The company was bought by South Pacific Pictures chief executive John Barnett and Vector Energy chairman Michael Stiassny.

'It's awesome. It's good to be back doing music and what we love doing … I wanted to let people know we're back in the game. I didn't want anybody else to take criticism or negativity from the first project. If there was any, then I would take it myself.'

Element of Surprise features Savage, Aaradhna, Mareko and two artists from the United States.

'We've been labelled a hip hop label for a long time but we love music in general. Whatever style – whether it be rhythm and blues, soul – we just love music.'

Brotha D says the label wants to increase its music catalogue and continue to showcase new talent.

Recent songs by Savage and Mareko have featured in blockbuster movies *Knocked Up* and *Super Bad*.

'One thing we've always tried to do with our music is build the catalogue so we can place songs into movies.'

Nurturing talent takes work but it is something Dawn Raid loves doing, he says. 'Most of these kids have come straight out of school or a garage and we have to develop them to become stars of the music community and these kids have to learn to deal with it.'

Dawn Raid will also release work from Beatrootz of Wellington, reggae group Sweet and Irie and the Deceptikonz.

DAWN RAID MUSIC LTD

This time around Andy and Brotha D have a better idea of where they want the company to go. 'Our focus will be a lot more direct than it was before. Before it was all over the place … We've put a budget down and understand that it all costs.'

October 2007

Senior Business Studies   ISBN 9780170215732

ACTIVITY

Review

- Identify the reasons why Tasty Pot could be considered to be a successful business after only one year of trading.

- Explain whether or not you think that Tasty Pot will be a sustainable business.

- How important have external factors been in the success of Tasty Pot?

- Given their difficulties, identify two reasons for Dawn Raid's success.

- Given the information in the case study, do you think that Dawn Raid will be a sustainable business?

- What skills and qualities has Brotha D shown in this case study?

Business formation

9

At the end of this unit you will be able to:

- Explain the important reasons for setting up a business.
- Describe and explain the advantages and disadvantages of different types of businesses.

'My first six years of business were hopeless. There were lots of times when I sat and said, "Why am I doing this? I will never make it. It is not going to happen. I should go out and get a real job." '

(George Lucas, entrepreneur and creator of *Star Wars*, owner of Lucas Film)

The table from Unit 1 is repeated below to remind us how important small business is in New Zealand. The number of small businesses constantly starting-up is a reflection of the strong enterprise culture that exists. Use the data to answer the questions that follow.

Number of employees	Number of businesses		Total employees	
	2010	2005	2010	2005
0	323,935	293,237	0	0
1-5	97,888	96,588	225,930	223,510
6-9	19,571	19,873	141,040	143,710
10-19	15,980	16,148	213,710	215,960
20-49	8,420	8,712	249,570	258,210
50-99	2,489	2,487	170,670	170,470
100+	2,063	1,972	888,980	842,830

ISBN 9780170215732

Senior Business Studies

ISBN 9780170215732

ACTIVITY

Review

- What percentage of total businesses in New Zealand is considered small?

- What percentage of the total workforce is accounted for by small businesses?

- Briefly explain any trends in the data from 2005 for both the number of businesses and total employees (workforce). Refer to the table on the previous page.

Discussion

- In Unit 1 we defined the term entrepreneur. Why do you think that entrepreneurs are so important to the economic welfare of New Zealand?

- Why do you think that so many New Zealanders wish to become entrepreneurs?

Reasons for setting up a small business

Before we look at different types of New Zealand businesses in more detail, we need to take a step back and think about why it is that so many New Zealanders start-up their own businesses and develop their entrepreneurial abilities in the first place:

- To become financially independent and sustainable if there are limited employment opportunities available in a particular geographic region.

- To pursue a passion or transform a hobby into a sustainable business idea and generate income.

- To exercise a degree of control over the 'work/life' balance and give greater flexibility.

- Having identified a new market (or gap), the entrepreneur wishes to create a new business to profitably fulfil these new wants and needs.

- There are significant tax advantages when creating a small business that operates from the owner's home.

- The apparent ease with which one can set up a business in New Zealand.

The last reason above may seem at odds with the others mentioned, however, one key factor in encouraging the enterprise culture in New Zealand is that it *actually is* one of the easiest countries in the world to set up a new business as shown in the following table (from *The Economist* publication 'Business Miscellany').

Country	Number of procedures required to set up and register a new business	Days for each procedure
New Zealand	2	12
United States	5	5
United Kingdom	6	8
Singapore	7	18
Kazakhstan	6	25
Nigeria	9	44
China	10	41
Paraguay	12	74
Indonesia	12	151

Research

• The above table was published in 2004. According to more recent figures, it is now even easier and quicker to start up a new business in New Zealand. (If a business has a turnover of less than $60,000 then it does not have to register for GST, making it even quicker to start-up a small business.) Update the information in this table. The Ministry of Economic Development and the IRD have very good informative websites. Students should also look at www.companies.govt.nz.

• Interview at least two small business owners to identify the reasons why they set up their business.

Thinking

• What are the implications for the New Zealand economy of it being able to start up and register new small businesses?

• What could be the impact on small business sustainability if a large number of new businesses try to enter a market at the same time?

Types of small business in New Zealand

The following table lists the three different types of small business entities – **sole trader, partnership and company** – and a description of their operations, taken from *Small Business* (2004).

Form	Ownership	Governance	Risks/liability	Legislation	Taxation
Sole trader	The business owner trades in their own name and they own the assets personally.	Sole trader is in control of the day to day running of the business and the strategic direction.	Unlimited liability and personal assets are at risk. Who will take over in the event of illness/death of the owner?	None specific to this business type.	Taxed at individual marginal rates. Highest is 33%.
Partnership	The partners own the assets according to their partnership ratios (as laid down in the agreement).	The partners operate the business in accordance with their own agreed structure.	Personal assets are at risk. They are jointly liable.	Partnership act 1908 but over-ridden by any new partnership agreement.	All income distributed to partners in their agreed ratios according to the agreement who are then taxed at personal marginal rates.
Company	Shareholders who each own a proportion of the assets in their particular shareholding ratio.	The shareholders appoint a board of directors. In very small companies usually the same people.	Limited to the assets of the company but can be varied depending on specific circumstances.	The Companies Act 1993 and any related legislation.	Company's profit taxed at 28%.

ISBN 9780170215732

Issues for small business owners

How does a small business owner decide which type of legal entity is most suitable? One way to find out involves asking a number of crucial questions:

- Which current government legislation applies to my business structure?
- How much official paperwork do I want or need to carry out?
- How do I wish to manage the business?
- What will be the implications for decision-making and management if new partners are introduced?
- Who will take over the business if the owner dies?
- How much personal liability and risk do I wish to experience?
- Do I wish to share profits and/or liability?

The Māori concept of **tūranga** can be applied here.

There are other difficult choices that must be made, namely the balance between managing risk, flexibility and liability. These three considerations have a direct impact on the final legal entity chosen.

Risk and flexibility vs liability

How much risk the business is willing to take needs to be balanced with the degree of liability experienced by the business owner.

In the case of the sole trader, the risk and opportunity costs of starting a new business could be considerable, however, the profits could potentially be unlimited.

Nevertheless, what will happen if the business fails? The owner may have to sell some of his or her assets to pay for the debts of the business, potentially leaving them without a home to live in. Are you willing to pursue your passion and put your own family's basic needs as collateral?

Imagine you have your own company. It has been created from your passion or hobby. Are you willing to share the business risk with others or do you wish to go it alone? You may have to give up some flexibility if you invite other people into the business. The disadvantage is that you have to share the rewards, however, if things go wrong you will each share the liability.

To see these points in action, let us return to a story of Real Groovy in Wellington (see page 36) and add a little more information about Mr Thomas, the sole trader.

ISBN 9780170215732

It will be the end of an era for Wellington's music lovers, but the end of a dream for Mr Thomas, the Whakatane-born, Waikato-bred owner of Real Groovy Wellington since 2008. Mr Thomas managed the shop since it opened in 1999, and mortgaged his house to buy the business after its parent company went into receivership.

He hopes to open a smaller record store if he can. But right now he is focused on shutting down Real Groovy and keeping hold of his house, which he shares with his wife and three kids.

Clearly Mr Thomas would not wish to jeopardise his family's security, but one of the issues for sole traders is that they have to raise funds in order to pursue their passion, and this usually means risking the family home as security.

Let us look at a fictitious case study that illustrates some of the points we have discussed above.

CASE STUDY

Alex's Cool Solution

Alex Johnson left school at 17 and decided to start up his own computer service business located 42 km north of Auckland city. Computers, gaming and film-making were his passion, and while at school he was regularly asked by both fellow students and teachers to help them with their computer problems.

Teachers often had particular problems with setting up computer and running new programs, whereas the students had very technical problems mostly around gaming (which only Alex and two of his friends, Jordan and Peter, knew how to solve). Faced with a growing number of requests, Alex advised stakeholders to go online and find out the answers to their questions using social networking sites, however they still came back to him for an answer. Alex was confident that although he had not conducted market research, his service could be transformed into a sustainable business following in the success of www.needanerd.co.nz.

Alex prepared a business plan and showed it to his parents. The business would initially be run from his own bedroom. He registered a business name,

'Alex's Cool Solutions (AJCS)' and obtained an IRD number. Without his own car, he decided to advertise himself only locally using local free newspapers and through his contacts from school.

AJCS became an instant success and Alex began to work 12 hour days just to satisfy and service his existing customers. It did not seem like work, but Alex became frustrated that he had very little or no time to spend on his film-making. Alex had been inspired by George Lucas and wanted to fulfil his lifelong dream of being an independent film-maker.

Frustration soon turned to anger. Alex felt that he was missing out on very large profits due to his lack of a car. AJCS had been invited to bid for a contract to help businesses in central Auckland with their computer issues. Alex would have to drive into the city daily and the local bus service was too infrequent. He needed new finance. Although AJCS had been successful it had not returned a sufficient profit to finance the purchase of a car.

Then Jordan and Peter called Alex, to see if he was interested in setting up a partnership. They could service the local market, leaving Alex the chance to develop his business in the city. Alex wanted to keep control of the business but he realised that he needed help. He also felt that Jordan and Peter were unreliable. He was unsure of his next move.

ACTIVITY

Review

- Explain the primary reason why Alex set up AJCS.

- Write down two advantages and two disadvantages for Alex setting up AJCS.

- Using the case study, identify the most appropriate type of business for Alex to set up AJCS.

- What risks, if any, is Alex taking?

- Why do you think that Alex created a business plan?

- Explain the advantages and disadvantages of promoting a business such as AJCS using social media networking sites.

- Advise Alex on what his next move should be.

Research

- For the sake of clarity the formation of trusts has been excluded from the types of small businesses in New Zealand table. Interested students may wish to find out for themselves the implications of structuring a small business using a family trust.

ISBN 9780170215732 Senior Business Studies

Sources of finance

At the end of this unit you will be able to:

- Identify funding options for business.
- Discuss factors that influence each finance option.

We saw from the previous unit involving Alex's Cool Solutions (AJCS) that funding options for small business are very important to consider, even given the risks. The small business owner, Alex, knew that increasing the number of other owners in the business would lead to new capital being available to help the business grow. And that the liability of the business would be spread around the other owners.

By introducing new partners, however, each owner would have to give up some of their control of AJCS, and perhaps some of the flexibility, as now each partner would have to be consulted if any of them wished to try something different.

Alternatively, to finance his new growth, Alex could have gone to a bank to ask for a loan. This is called **debt financing**. He would be able to keep full control of the business, but would now have a much bigger exposure to liability. If the loan is secured (or guaranteed) against his parent's house, for example, then the implications for both Alex and his parents if AJCS got into financial difficulties would be considerable.

The importance of finance

Even new start-ups, which have been created from the bedroom such as AJCS, need finance. The type of finance required by a business will depend on what the finance is needed for.

Before we look at the main types of finance available to small and large businesses, we need to consider two important terms: **fixed** and **current assets**.

Senior Business Studies   ISBN 9780170215732

A **fixed asset** (or capital) is usually a piece of equipment that is held by a business for a long period of time (longer than a year), and includes items such as the premises, machinery, fixtures and fittings and vehicles.

A **current asset** is usually held by the business for less than a year, and is required to cover the short-term financing needs such as the purchase of stock or raw materials for sale, or to pay suppliers and other expenses.

Current asset finance is sometimes called working capital, and it is vital in order to make the fixed assets become more productive. Without working capital, fixed assets will stand idle and be unproductive.

Working capital

Working capital is a vital but poorly understood concept in business. It is also known by the terms day-to-day or circulating capital. Working capital has a very important role to play in cashflow management and is an important factor in planning, especially for new businesses.

Poor cashflow planning is one the main reasons why new businesses fail in the first two years of operation. We will look at cashflow forecasts and management in a later unit (see pages 88-93).

The working capital cycle

Let us take a very straightforward example of a sausage manufacturer to see how this working capital cycle can work. We will assume that the sausage firm pays for its raw materials very quickly in cash and that all customers will pay on time. (Anyone with any business experience will agree that this is very rarely the case!)

Senior Business Studies   ISBN 9780170215732

Work capital cycle

Firm receives an order for 5000 sausages from a supermarket.

Firm pays for raw ingredients in order to make the sausages. Two workers begin the process.

The firm produces 5000 sausages and more workers package them. Firms pay its suppliers of raw materials and sends out a bill (or invoice) to customers.

The firm delivers the sausages and the customers pay the invoice.

The sausage manufacturer pays its workers and then receives a new order (hopefully) to make more sausages and the process begins again.

If we introduce the term 'credit', or the ability to delay or receive payment for a certain time period, the working capital cycle will change. Let's assume that the sausage manufacturer allows credit for 30 days to its customers, and is allowed 28 days to pay for its raw materials, things become a little more interesting ...

ACTIVITY

Discussion

- What happens if all customers do not pay on time?
- What happens if the customers' customers do not pay on time?
- What do you think we mean by the term interdependence?
- Why is it very important for businesses to be aware of interdependence and its impact on the working capital cycle?

ISBN 9780170215732

Senior Business Studies

Funding options for small and large businesses

By understanding how fixed and current assets and the working capital cycle works, we are now in a position to look at possible sources of funding for small businesses as it starts up, if it has problems with working capital, or if it wishes to grow.

Remember! The choice of finance used should be directly related to its purpose. That means short-term finance for short-term needs, and long-term finance for long-term needs.

Consider the possible sources of funding for four different purposes outlined in table below.

Funding purpose	Possible source of finance	Discussion
Starting up the business	Owners own savings or from an inheritance.	A very popular way to start-up a business but needs to be sufficient to provide for both fixed assets (if required) and current assets such as stock of products for sale. (Referred to as Inventory.)
	A new mortgage on existing house.	As above but given unlimited liability on the part of the owner, the family's main asset is now under threat if the business gets into financial difficulties.
	Borrowing from the bank in the form of a bank loan.	The bank manager will require a business plan (see Unit 11) and this will take time and resources to put together.
	Government sponsored schemes from the Ministry of Economic Development, for example.	A number of schemes are available to start-ups. Again the amounts involved are small

ISBN 9780170215732

Senior Business Studies

Funding purpose	Possible source of finance	Discussion
Growing the business, and advice and support	Angel Investors or the use of Incubators such as the Icehouse (Auckland) or Creative HQ (Wellington).	An ability to use experienced advisors who may be able to impart invaluable advice at low cost. However, they will want a say in how the business is run.
	Micro-finance sourced from overseas via the Internet.	Small in New Zealand but increasingly popular in the developing world to help new start-ups. Only small amounts of money may be available.
The need to make the working capital cycle run smoothly	Extending the bank overdraft.	This is an expensive way to finance working capital and it should be short term only.
	Offering discounts to customers for prompt payment.	May act as an incentive to pay early but amount received will be less.
	Use of 'debt factor' company if customers cannot or refuse to pay.	Will get only a fraction of the final debt amount but useful to help with cashflow.
Finance for growth to purchase new fixed assets such as capital equipment and vehicles	More bank loans may be required	A new business and strategic plan will need to be drawn up. Banks will require a thorough review of current and future business activity.
	More easily obtained if the company has limited liability or is quoted on the NZ Stock Exchange.	This method can raise large amounts of capital quickly but there may be the issue of giving up some control through diluted ownership if shares bought by outside investors.
	Sale and leaseback.	A new method where businesses may sell an asset but then hire it back without the direct responsibility of ownership. This has become a very popular way to finance large s ICT or computer networks that may become obsolete or out of date very quickly and thus reduce in value very quickly. The latest IT facilities can be incorporated with reduced financial exposure.

Senior Business Studies   ISBN 9780170215732

The following case study looks at a growing small business and incorporates some financial issues and topics from previous chapters.

Humble sausage gains panache

Branco's Sausages is the brand name of the Auckland-based family company Bramax. Established in 1995 by the South African immigrant, the business has grown substantially as consumers have looked at purchasing higher quality sausages.

'We wanted to provide something a little different to the market full of mass-produced sausages. We have created a European styled product, a true boerewors [which means farmer's sausage], and to take that delicatessen style of sausage and make it widely available to the supermarket shopper,' Max Poznanovich owner said.

The business is a family affair with mum Juanita on the payroll and the only other staff members being a brother and sister team who work in the processing room.

Max Poznanovich had been a butcher in Capetown before moving to New Zealand, but he had no plans to set up a meat firm here. But when people discovered he could make the traditional sausages and biltong (dried beef) he got lots of requests. He had a job packing decoders for Sky TV, but people used to come and ask him to make boerewors because they knew he was South African.

Branco's now supplies 60 North Island supermarkets, but marketing the product has been a big job. 'We've taken a foreign product into a new market and relentlessly promoted it … because it's got a strange name, a funny colour and is priced higher than other sausages, instore demonstrations where people can actually taste them has been the way to go,' Poznanovich said.

Initially the business shared premises but last September the family moved it to their own building. 'We've grown by putting money back into the business and have used only as much as our capital allowed. We're quite concerned about having too much debt but we've stretched ourselves a bit to get into the new premises,' Poznanovich said.

He's confident it's the right move. The company broke even in its second year and while there are now more bills to cover, there's also been a 40% increase in turnover in the past year. The company has also just launched what it says is the first supermarket sausage (a boerewors style) to be granted the Heart Foundation's tick of approval.

ISBN 9780170215732

'We don't aim to compete with what's there. We're small, so we see a gap in the market and fill it,' he said. 'Because we're small, we're more flexible so we can meet the market.' New Zealand is a nation of sausage lovers with 31.5% of us indulging at least once per week. Aucklanders alone eat an estimated 50.8 million sausages a year.

February 2004

ACTIVITY

Review

- From the case study, identify how Branco's have demonstrated:

  - Innovation.

  - Risk-taking.

- Explain how Branco's have financed their growth and innovation. Fully explain why you think they chose this source of finance.

- Describe one advantage and one disadvantage from so many members of the same family being involved with Branco's.

- Given your answer above, suggest an alternative source of finance for Branco's Sausages. How likely is it that the family would take up this funding option?

- Assume that Branco's Sausages decide to find a business partner who has significant financé but no knowledge of the sausage industry. What do you think could be the impact on innovation and risk-taking at Branco's?

Business planning and decision-making

11

At the end of this unit you will be able to:

- Understand and explain the need for decision-making in business.

- Develop and refine a business plan.

This unit has links to Level 1 Internal Assessment AS 90842 and Level 2 AS 90848. Level 2 requires students to plan an activity involving their community, carry out one cycle of the activity, then review their performance and refine their plan based on their experiences. More information about the type of business plan required for these standards can be found at www.tki.org.nz.

The need for decision-making

We know that business owners need to make decisions. Some of these may be day-to-day or short-term tactical decisions, which may only involve a few individuals within the organisation, such as:

- How to pay for raw materials.

- How to deal with a stakeholder complaint.

- The purchase of new fixed or current assets.

Senior Business Studies   ISBN 9780170215732

However, some decisions may involve the whole organisation:

- Should we develop a new aim to expand production into China?
- Should we restructure the business and organise ourselves by department or brand?
- Should we relocate our manufacturing department to Thailand?

Whatever decision needs to be made, planning will be required.

A decision-making model

Many students will be familiar with the generic decision-making framework (below). It is taught in many schools in New Zealand as part of the life skills or financial literacy programme. It can be applied in any situation where a decision needs to be made, whether it is made by an organisation in business and management, or by an individual in purchasing a new mobile phone.

The model assumes that decision-making is a scientific process, and is useful in that it can be applied in a number of business and management contexts. It is outlined below.

Set objectives for the organisation with the requirement that a new decision needs to be taken to fulfil this objective.

Gather data relevant to the decision being taken. Identify possible internal and external constraints which may impact on your decision.

Analyse the information and identify suitable courses of action. Analyse each of the alternatives as objectively as possible. May need guidance by a third party.

Choose a course of action.

Implement and decide on time frame for review.

Review and if necessary undertake more market research and acquire more data. Objectives may have to be reset in the light of new information.

Senior Business Studies   ISBN 9780170215732

Once the decision is made, it is critical to review it. Depending on the decision, a firm may wish to:

- Look at sales figures to predict the outcome of a new marketing strategy.

- Consult stakeholders to predict the impact of the decision and whether initial objectives have been satisfied.

- Conduct additional market research, both primary and secondary, to view the perception of the firm (if it has entered a new overseas market).

Failure to review the final decision may leave the firm looking 'bad' in the eyes of stakeholders (especially shareholders), especially in the event that mistakes occur, or if sales or profit forecasts do not meet expectations.

Another, more fundamental reason, to review performance is that if the company has made a mistake it would be irresponsible to repeat it. Failure to plan once may be an oversight, but to do so twice and not learn from the mistake is unforgivable in business.

Why do we plan?

'Those who fail to plan, plan to fail.'

(Anon)

A plan is a programme or scheme worked out in order to achieve an objective. Planning is the first step in the management process. It is an area that many young entrepreneurs overlook or neglect to take seriously.

Planning can be carried out formally or informally. (For the purposes of this course we will look at more formal plans. The Level 1 and 2 Business internal assessment activities should be conducted as part of a group project and include contributions for all team members.)

Different types of plans

The type of business plan needed will depend on the objectives of the organisation, the purpose of the plan and its intended audience.

For example, a plan that is aimed at developing a long-term strategy for growth for a large business in an overseas market involving millions of dollars of finance will look very different to a plan aimed at providing a hockey team at a school with an opportunity to promote and sell sausages at a fundraising event. Nevertheless, both need to be taken seriously.

ISBN 9780170215732

Senior Business Studies

What should a business plan contain?

- The objectives of the organisation and, if possible, their long term strategic vision.

- A review of existing or potential firms in competition, and the current state of the external environment.

- Who or where is the target market and how was this target market discovered?

- A review of the market research carried out to date, and additional research that will need to be carried out to refine the plan (an important point for Level 2 students).

- What resources – human and non-human – will be needed and what will they cost? Will there be any additional human resources required? Will they be full or part time staff? Will there be any management issues to consider?

- If it is a new business start-up, what will be the fixed assets and working capital requirements?

- If the plan is going to involve a strategic change, what will be the impacts on internal and external stakeholders?

Beyond the main business plan, an outline of the **marketing approach** should be provided:

- How is the new product or service going to be promoted?

- How will it be distributed?

- What is going to be the likely price of the product?

- What is the forecasted number of sales?

If a plan looking to **secure funding** is going to be presented to a stakeholder, such as an investor or bank manger, forecasts of potential profit and cashflow must be included:

- Budgets for revenue items such as promotion, training or recruitment.

- Timelines will need to be included and (importantly for Level 2 students) show how the plan will be reviewed. Suggestions of what action could be taken if initial sales forecasts are lower than expected should be provided.

Planning for a tactical objective

Returning to the example of Alex's business AJCS (see Unit 9), let us assume that he wishes to write a quick business plan for a bank manager. In this business plan, Alex will have to show how he intends to use the new company car to benefit AJCS. Draft a number of ideas that the plan will need to cover. The first one has been carried out for you.

Senior Business Studies   ISBN 9780170215732

Objective: Alex wishes to raise finance to purchase a new business company car.

- The amount of finance required and the length of time he will need to pay the money back.

- A forecast of the number of customers he will be expecting to satisfy with his new service away from his local market.

- A list of fixed and variable running costs of a new car.

- Whether Alex intends to buy the car outright and own it (fixed asset), or whether he will lease the car and treat it as a revenue item (working capital).

Review

- Alex wishes to borrow money to finance a possible move into a new market – the selling of computers using a retail store.

- Alex wishes to expand AJCS into an overseas market and wants to create a website promotion his services.

- What similarities or differences, if any, do you notice between the brief plans if any?

- Explain the importance of Alex gaining as much accurate information as possible.

- Why is it difficult for Alex to obtain accurate information about future sales and costs?

SWOT analysis

Before a plan is created, many businesses carry out a **SWOT** analysis, which is a technique designed to find out the current standing of the business in terms of its Strengths, Weaknesses, Opportunities and Threats:

- Strengths and weakness are said to be **internal** to the business, and to some degree the business does have some control over these.

  Possible strengths include sustainability or a creative product. Weaknesses may focus on problems around recruiting staff for specific roles.

ISBN 9780170215732 Senior Business Studies

- Opportunities and threats are said to be **external** to the organisation and outside the control of the business. They are linked to the external environment in which the business operates.

  - An opportunity could be releasing the product into a new or unknown market, or a threat could be the emergence of a new rival company in the local market.

Disney in the late 1970s: SWOT in action

After the death of its founder in 1966, the Disney company felt that it needed to look closely at its operations and so conducted a very thorough SWOT analysis. Here are some brief details.

 Strengths

- Very strong brand known globally and built on family values.
- Animation techniques in cartoons and live action movies.
- Theme parks creating a vision of the future world envisaged by Walt Disney.

 Weaknesses

- Run by the same family since the 1930s – a lack of fresh thinking?
- Reliance on job production (see Unit 17). It is expensive and time consuming to produce animated cartoons.

 Opportunities

- Theme parks in other countries to capitalise the strength of the global brand.
- A move into action films.
- Trying to change a once-in-a-lifetime visit into a more regular event.

 Threats

- Competition from film-makers in similar markets, such as George Lucas.
- Use of technology to make films.
- Threat of home video taking people away from the movie theatres.

The SWOT analysis provided Disney with an opportunity to implement improvements to their operation. This type of analysis is usually carried out by an independent expert (such as a management consultant), rather than the company themselves, to avoid problems of bias.

ISBN 9780170215732

Senior Business Studies

The plan that emerged from this process was a new long-term strategy. It was probably refined and updated many times once the recommendation from the SWOT analysis had been undertaken.

Action taken by Disney:

- Built Tokyo Disneyland (1983) and Euro Disney (1992) theme parks.

- Took over an independent movie company (Miramax) to produce more drama films.

- Reduced the number of animated cartoon movies to produce higher quality movies less often such as *Aladdin* and *Beauty and the Beast*.

- Entered in a joint venture with a new company called Pixar using new technology to create movies such as *Toy Story*. Bought Pixar in 2006 for $US 7.4 billion.

Breakeven analysis

Another important part of a business plan, especially for new SMEs, is the use of breakeven analysis. Although we noted earlier that business planning should be a formal process, we also need to understand whether or not a decision we wish to make has the potential to earn profits or generate sufficient sales.

Unless there are very different business objectives, such as raising awareness of a specific issue, most decision-makers wish to know whether or not their idea will yield profit. The technique used here is called the **breakeven**.

Definition

Breakeven is the output at which revenue equals costs. In other words, no loss or profit is made.

- Total revenue = price x quantity
- Total costs = fixed costs + variable costs
- Fixed costs do not change with output e.g. rent
- Variable costs vary directly with output e.g. materials
- Profit = total revenue – total costs

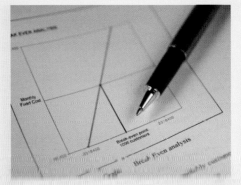

ISBN 9780170215732

Senior Business Studies

A typical breakeven chart looks like this:

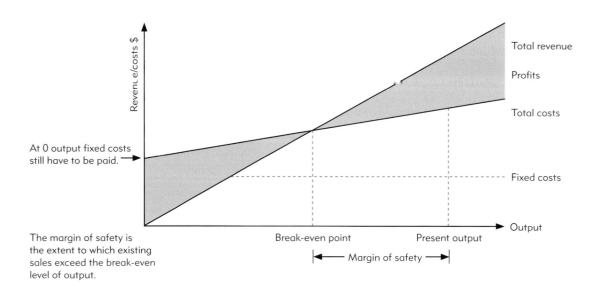

At 0 output fixed costs still have to be paid. →

Revenue/costs $ (vertical axis)

Output (horizontal axis)

Total revenue
Profits
Total costs
Fixed costs

Break-even point   Present output

|← Margin of safety →|

The margin of safety is the extent to which existing sales exceed the break-even level of output.

Given that the diagram may be drawn inaccurately or the intersection point between total costs and total revenue may not be clear by eye, it can be useful to confirm the breakeven point using the following formula:

$$\text{breakeven quantity calculated} = \frac{\text{fixed costs}}{\text{contribution}}$$

CASE STUDY

ARC paid $2.9m for David Beckham

The Auckland Regional Council spent $2.91 million on travel, accommodation and promotion for the ill-fated football match between David Beckham's LA Galaxy and the Oceania All Stars, which ended up losing $1.7m a report has shown.

ARC chief executive Peter Winder said no specific amount had been spent on bringing Beckham to Auckland but it had been hoped that his 'superstar status would make the event as big a success as the 2007 match in Wellington.

The proposal for LA Galaxy versus an Oceania All Stars team was viewed as a concept devised so that a wide range of people of differing ethnic descent such as Asian and Pacific peoples.

The 'breakeven' crowd needed was 25,000 and considering Wellington attracted 31,800 people to a Beckham event in 2007, the report said it was unlikely that this crowd size would not be achieved.

A profit of $484,350 was expected if 30,000 tickets were sold.

However, on the night a crowd of only 16,587 turned out, and 'a portion of these were complimentary (free) or were offered in a two-for-one deal, resulting in lower revenue.'

Mr Winder's review of what went wrong highlights the following factors leading to the loss of $1.79 million. The ticket price was too high, the marketing ineffective and the Oceania team was not good enough to be considered a creditable opposition, which failed to attract fans. Sales revenue was 70% below target.

February 2009

ACTIVITY

Discussion

- The first football match involving LA Galaxy in 2007 was a financial success. Discuss whether or not mistakes were made in deciding to hold a second match in Auckland the following year.

- What other data (apart from the breakeven data) would you need to find out whether or not the LA Galaxy vs Oceania match could have been a success?

Inquiry

- Carry out a SWOT analysis on yourself!

- Having carried out the analysis, what action should you take to improve your performance at school?

12 Financial records

At the end of this unit you will be able to:

- Outline why businesses keep financial records.
- Understand the need and importance of financial records for business success and decision-making.

If we recall one of the early units on sole traders and small businesses in New Zealand, you will remember one common reason why so many small businesses become unsustainable and do not survive the first year of trading is poor or inaccurate financial book keeping.

In this unit we will look at the main types of financial records that small businesses need to collect and, importantly, explain the reason why. We will focus on the balance sheet and profit and loss account, then in the next unit look at the cashflow cycle.

In Unit 11 we saw the importance of planning and why some firms may use breakeven charts to aid their decision-making. However, it would be impossible to run a business on a breakeven output alone. Businesses both large and small need to consider all aspects of their financial performance – current financial position and future cash needs – if the business is to be sustainable.

CASE STUDY

Skate shop grabs more top gongs

You know you've got a loyal following when a regular keeps a newspaper clipping about your Small Business of the Year gong.

ISBN 9780170215732

It's the kind of faithful customer base Manukau skateboard and snowboard retailer, Boardertown, has worked hard to cultivate.

Created six years ago when founders Matthew Traynor and Daniel McClean were just 19, the Botany Town Centre store has now been named Westpac Manukau Small Business of the Year two years running.

The business has grown 1500% from humble beginnings at its first shop in Howick, and has focused on putting robust accounting, human resource and marketing systems in place to enable this growth to take place.

The business has also kept a very keen eye on the external environment and the nature of the retail market they are in. Girls' fashion, for example, was a growing part of the business but constantly changing.

Boardertown's main trade is in skateboards, followed by snowboards and an emerging market in wakeboards. It sources overseas product itself and goes through distributors.

Despite a competitive market and weak economic conditions and a 16% downturn at the Botany mall in the past two years, Boardertown's year-on-year revenue was up 13% with gross profit up 35%, Guy said.

He puts Boardertown's success down to its impressive growth and financial control amid difficult times.

'We are keen to open more stores but we require new sources of finance to do so. It is important that we get our financial records looking right, such as our balance sheet, so we can attract suitable investors.'

Committed to having a positive impact on community, a recent highlight for them is the new Barry Curtis skate park. Guy has helped lobby for the park for 10 years.

'For me, when I was a 15-year-old kid it's the thing you always dream of having, your own skateboard shop.'

November 2010

Review

- Identify two reasons for the success of Boardertown.

- Explain why 'keeping robust accounting, human resource and marketing systems' is important for a new business start-up.

- Identify and explain a suitable source of funding for Boardertown to help finance its expansion plans.

- Explain one financial benefit to Boadertown from supporting the building of a new skate park in the local area.

ACTIVITY

ISBN 9780170215732

Senior Business Studies

The importance of financial records

Financial accounts provide an invaluable source of information to help control the business and assist in decision making now and in the future.

Financial accounts are also required to satisfy certain legal requirements of operating a business, especially with respect to any tax liabilities owing on business profits.

These records are needed to provide 'transparency' on the company's financial position to external stakeholders such as potential investors, suppliers and lenders.

Key financial accounts

New Zealand students are being increasingly exposed to financial literacy programmes in primary and intermediate schools, and in pre-NCEA classes at secondary, therefore a full treatment of financial accounting is not given here. Instead we will use one company's set of financial accounts to demonstrate how they can be constructed, and their use for management. (The documents for Apple Corporation have been edited to tone down some of the technical jargon.)

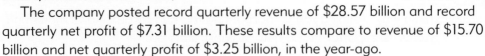

Apple reports third quarter results: all-time record revenue and earnings

iPhone Sales Grow 142%; iPad Sales Grow 183%

Apple today announced financial results for its fiscal 2011 third quarter ended June 25, 2011.

The company posted record quarterly revenue of $28.57 billion and record quarterly net profit of $7.31 billion. These results compare to revenue of $15.70 billion and net quarterly profit of $3.25 billion, in the year-ago.

Gross margin was 41.7% compared to 39.1% in the year-ago quarter.

International sales accounted for 62% of the quarter's revenue.

The company sold 20.34 million iPhones in the quarter, representing 142% unit growth over the year-ago quarter.

Apple sold 9.25 million iPads during the quarter, a 183% unit increase over the year-ago quarter.

Senior Business Studies   ISBN 9780170215732

The company sold 3.95 million Macs during the quarter, a 14% unit increase over the year-ago quarter.

Apple sold 7.54 million iPods, a 20% unit decline from the year-ago quarter.

'We are extremely pleased with our performance which drove quarterly cashflow from operations of $11.1 billion, an increase of 131% year-over-year,' said Peter Oppenheimer, Apple's CFO.

Apple designs iMacs, the best personal computers in the world, along with OS X, iLife, iWork and professional software. Apple leads the digital music revolution with its iPods and iTunes online store. Apple has reinvented the mobile phone with its revolutionary iPhone and App Store, and has recently introduced iPad 2 which is defining the future of mobile media and computing devices.

Profit and Loss Account for Apple (simplified)

	Three Months Ended		Nine Months Ended	
	June 25, 2011	June 26, 2010	June 25, 2011	June 26, 2010
Net sales	$ 28, 571	$ 15,700	$ 79,979	$ 44,882
Cost of sales	16, 649	9,564	47,541	26,710
Gross margin	11, 922	6,136	32,438	18,172
Operating profit:				
Research and development	628	464	1,784	1,288
Selling, general and administrative	1,915	1,438	5,574	3,946
Total operating expenses	2,543	1,902	7,358	5,234
Operating profit (net)	9,379	4,234	25,080	12,938
Other income and expense	172	58	334	141
Income before provision for income taxes	2,243	1,039	6,115	3,374
Net profit	$ 7,308	$ 3,253	$ 19,299	$ 9,705

ISBN 9780170215732

Senior Business Studies

Review

- Define the terms in bold in the profit and loss account.

- Why do you think a company such as Apple spends significant sums of money on research and development?

- What other financial information would you need in order to judge the success of Apple's profits compared to other technology companies?

- From the information above, explain how successful you think Apple has been from June 2010 to June 2011.

- Why has the number of iPods sold decreased by 20%?

Research

- Apple has launched a new service allowing Apple consumers the chance to store all of their media files such as movies, music and photos in one place to be access anytime, anywhere on any computer. This service is called iCloud. How do you think that iCloud will impact on sales of Apple's products and services?

Balance Sheet for Apple (simplified)

	June 25, 2011	September 25, 2010
ASSETS		
Current assets:		
Cash and cash equivalents	$ 12,091	$ 11,261
Short-term marketable investments..	16,304	14,359
Accounts receivable, less allowances of $55 in each period	6,102	5,510
Stock	889	1,051
Other current assets...	1,892	5,369
Total current assets	46,898	41,678
Long-term marketable securities...	47,761	25,391
Property, plant and equipment, net	6,749	4,768
Goodwill	741	741
Acquired intangible assets, net..	1,169	342
Other assets..	3,440	2,263
Total assets...	$ 106,758	$ 75,183

ISBN 9780170215732

Liabilities and Shareholders' Equity for Apple (simplified)

Current liabilities:

Accounts payable..	$ 15,270	$ 12,015
Accrued expenses	7,597	5,723
Deferred revenue..	3,992	2,984
Total current liabilities..	26,859	20,722
Deferred revenue – non-current...	1,407	1,139
Other non-current liabilities	9,149	5,531
Total liabilities...	37,415	27,392

Commitments:

Shareholders' equity	12,715	10,668
Retained earnings	56,239	37,169
Accumulated other comprehensive income/(loss)..................	389	(46)
Total shareholders' equity..	69,343	47,791
Total liabilities and shareholders' equity	$ 106,758	$ 75,183

ACTIVITY

Review

- Define the terms used in bold in the balance sheet.

- Why do you think that businesses provide more than one year's worth of financial information in a balance sheet?

- Apple's balance sheet appears to be very healthy. What other financial information would you require before making an accurate judgment on the health of the company? (Level 2 students should link their answer to the state of external environments in the global economy.)

Thinking

- Can you explain any possible reason why a company such as Apple has far less capital invested in fixed assets than working capital invested in current assets?

Senior Business Studies   ISBN 9780170215732

Care around the use of financial accounts

Financial accounts have a number of important uses and we must always be careful when using them.

We have to trust that the figures offer a 'true and fair view' of the business. Unfortunately a number of scandals involving finance companies using false accounting records have shown that they can be misused. In one particular case, customers were encouraged to invest only to find out that some of the figures presented were false and, worse still, that senior managers had perpetuated a significant fraud. The film *Enron: The Smartest Guys in the Room* depicts the true story of one of the most appalling modern financial scandals.

It must be remembered that financial information is only accurate on the day it was published. The balance sheet only reveals a 'snapshot' of a business financial position on a particular moment in time, and could easily change the following trading day.

Finally, and linked to this idea, is that financial information does not tend to consider the external environment. Tough economic conditions in some markets may lead to financial performance looking rather shaky, when in fact a small increase in sales in a competitive market could actually represent a great achievement. This point is illustrated in a case study (below) of a retail business closer to home.

CASE STUDY >>>

JB Hi-Fi profits soar 26pc

Electronics retailer JB Hi-Fi has reported a 26% increase in full-year profit, and says it expects to grow sales by 17% in the current year.

JB Hi-Fi reported net profit in 2009/10 of $NZ149m, up from $A94.438 million in 2008/09.

JB Hi-Fi said it expected 'FY11 to be another good year of sales and earnings growth.'

In the financial year 2010, JB Hi-Fi opened 23 stores, the largest number it ever has opened in a year, and it expected to open a further 18 stores in 2010/11 across Australia and New Zealand.

August 2010

One year later ...

JB Hi-Fi posts smaller profit but upbeat on growth

JB Hi-Fi has reported a 7.55% decline in full-year net profit and indicates the market is expected to remain challenging. The uncertain economic outlook is not helping.

The company said net profit for the 12 months to June 30, 2011, was $A109.7 million ($136.8 million), down from $A118.65 million the previous year.

Revenue rose 8.35% to $A2.96 billion.

'We are pleased with our results in what has been a challenging period for retail,' Smart said.

August 2011

ACTIVITY

Review

- Briefly describe JB Hi-Fi's financial performance for 2009/10 and 2010/11.

- Sales revenue increased between 2010 and 2011 by 8.35%, yet profits fell. Explain what you think could have caused this to occur.

- What other information would you require to help judge whether JB Hi-Fi had performed well in 2010/11?

- Should JB Hi-Fi be pleased with its financial results?

- Using this case study, explain why we must be careful when taking other non-financial factors into account to assess financial performance.

Senior Business Studies   ISBN 9780170215732

13 The cashflow cycle

At the end of this unit you will be able to:

- Describe and understand the importance of the cashflow cycle.
- Draw up a simple cashflow forecast for a small business.

In an earlier unit we looked at the idea of the working capital cycle involving a sausage manufacturer – the working capital cycle allows businesses to generate good and services to be sold at a profit.

Then in the previous unit we saw the success of the Apple Corporation in terms of its financial performance, its profit/loss and balance sheet. Apple clearly has a good deal of cash at its disposal. (It was estimated to have more cash than the US government in early August 2011!)

Senior Business Studies   ISBN 9780170215732

Cash Statement of Apple (simplified)

	Nine Months Ended	
	June 25, 2011	September 25, 2010
Cash and cash equivalents, beginning of the period	$ 11,261	$ 5,263
Operating activities:		
Net income...	19,299	9,705
Cash generated by operating activities – after adjustments.......	27,100	12,912
Investing activities:		
Purchases of investments	(75,133)	(41,318)
Proceeds from sale of marketable securities.........................	50,697	33,806
Payments made in connection with business takeover	0	(615)
Payments for acquisition of property, plant and equipment ..	(2,615)	(1,245)
Payments for acquisition of intangible assets	(266)	(63)
Other	34	(36)
Cash used in investing activities	(27,283)	(9,471)
Financing activities:		
Proceeds from issuance of shares	577	733
Cash generated by all financing activities....................	1,013	1,001
Increase in cash and cash equivalents..	830	4,442
Cash and cash equivalents, end of the period	$ 12,091	$ 9,705

Review

- Describe generally how Apple has spent its cash. Do you think that shareholders would be pleased?

Working capital and the cashflow cycle

Unit 10 demonstrated that in order for a business to meet its responsibilities (to pay bills and wages, and order supplies), it has to receive revenue (cash) from its customers.

A company could ask for credit when it buys raw materials, however, even that is just another bill which will must be paid eventually.

We have also been introduced to the concept of interdependence. In terms of managing the cashflow cycle, an understanding of interdependence is crucial. In a business context, interdependence refers to fact that businesses have to rely on each other in order to survive. Let us consider the following scenario.

ISBN 9780170215732

Senior Business Studies

- Assume that in a small community there are four businesses: A, B, C, D.

- A supplies materials to B on credit and gives 31 days to pay. A receives supplies on credit from D and is given 30 days to pay.

- B processes the materials and sell them to C, giving 29 days to pay. C produces the final goods and tries to sell them in the local market.

- C finds it difficult to sell all of the goods, and a few days before payment to B is due calls the manager of B to say that they need a few extra days.

- B calls A. (Can you guess what might happen?)

- Failure by C to not to sell its goods for cash implies that, following the line of interdependence, A, B and D may all suffer from cashflow problems as a result.

- If this problem continues then A, B and D (and C!) could be forced out of business.

The importance of cashflow management

Managing cashflow is one of the most important aspects of financial management, and is the most common reason for small business failure.

To manage cashflow effectively, small businesses need to continually review their current and future cash position.

Even if a small business is given an opportunity to earn significant profits by accepting a larger customer order, it can still struggle if it fails to plan its cashflow needs adequately.

The diagram below illustrates the importance of cashflow management even before proceeds from a successful order are received.

Cashflow for small firm accepting a profitable $50,000 order

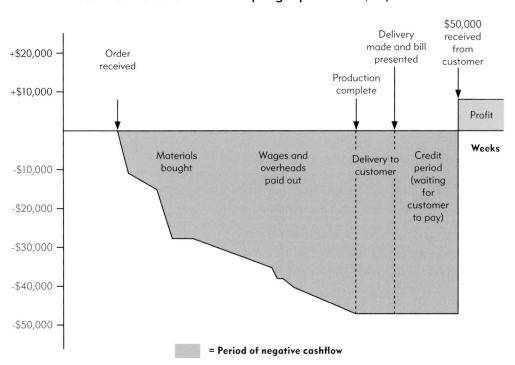

= Period of negative cashflow

ISBN 9780170215732

Cashflow forecasting: looking into the future

In addition to the balance sheet (Statement of Financial Position) and the profit and loss account (Statement of Financial Performance), another very important document for stakeholders of both small and large businesses is the cashflow forecast.

An example of a small business planning its cashflow needs (money coming in and going out) for the last half of the year is given on the next page. Use it to answer the questions that follow.

Typical cashflow forecast from June 20XX to Nov 20XX

Item	June	July	Aug	Sept	Oct	Nov
Opening balance						
Cash inflows						
Cash from customers						
Sale of assets						
Total cash available						
Cash outflows						
Rent						
Rates						
Materials						
Wages						
Total cash outflows						
Cash available – cash outflows						
Closing balance						

ACTIVITY

Review

- You are given the following information from AJCS (Alex's Cool Solutions). Use the data to answer the questions below.

> The date is the first of June.
>
> - Opening balance on June 1 = 1,000
>
> - Cash inflows from customers are expected to be $800 in June Increasing by $100 a month, until October when cash inflows from customers are expected to increase by $200 and by $400 in November
>
> - Old computers were sold In August and October for $100 in each month

Senior Business Studies   ISBN 9780170215732

Cash outflows are expected to be:

Rent	= $400 per month
Rates	= $100 per month
Wages paid	= $400 per month. In November, a pre-Christmas bonus will be paid doubling the wage
Computer spare parts	= $50 per month

Quarterly insurance is to be paid in June and September at $300 per month

- Draw up the cashflow forecast for AJCS from June to November.

- Comment on the cash position/forecast of AJCS expected in November.

- AJCS manager Alex believes that the forthcoming Christmas trading period will be slow. Advise Alex on what action he should take, given your final figure closing balance figure.

- Explain why cashflow forecasting is an important planning document for a small business such as AJCS.

- Identify two problems in using cashflow forecasts.

Problems with the cashflow cycle

Every type of business is vulnerable to changes in the cashflow cycle. Read the case study below and use it to answer the questions that follow.

CASE STUDY

Apprentice New Zealand boss in cash crisis

The Apprentice New Zealand star Terry Serepisos is being chased by creditors and is struggling to pay about $2 million in unpaid rates and ground rents to Wellington City Council.

A *Dominion Post* investigation has learnt that the council has met regularly with Mr Serepisos – but he has yet to see the substantial debt.

It is understood Mr Serepisos has told the council he is struggling to pay – and if the council takes action to recover money it could jeopardise the Wellington Phoenix football franchise he owns.

The *Dominion Post* has learnt the council has offered repeated extensions at meetings, which have included chief executive Garry Poole, amid growing concerns at the mounting debt.

The council is believed to have already provided Mr Serepisos with extra time to pay his rates because of potential repercussions for the Phoenix and for other organisations that do business with him.

Though Mr Serepisos has made some payments in the past year, it is understood he owes about $2 million. Local councils have the legal ability to approach banks that hold a mortgage on a property to demand payment when the owner fails to do so.

Mr Serepisos refused to discuss any aspect of his rates yesterday, saying it was 'confidential'. He said that, like any property developer, he had been affected by the recession: 'There is a global crisis here, I am certainly not immune the global crisis.' He was owed 'millions', including $450,000 in accommodation from the stalled movie *Kingdom Co* and $1.6m from a failed construction company.

'People owing me money puts a strain on cashflow as well. It is a domino effect right across the board. If he can't pay you, you can't pay him, that sort of thing … It is not just me, guys, it is the whole world. All I'm saying is I'm not immune to the global crisis. People owe me a lot of money.'

Mr Serepisos said he had spent vast sums promoting Wellington, bankrolling the Phoenix and working with several charities and the community.

'I'm pouring in millions and millions of dollars to promote this city and doing all these things I do. And I feel a little disheartened that a handful of people are taking pot shots at me.'

Mr Serepisos owns several companies including 79 Manners Street Ltd, Century City Developments Ltd, Century City Ltd, Century City Football Ltd and New Millennium Design.

It has been reported that debts ranging from $158,000 to $71,000 related to those companies have been referred to a debt collection company.

April 2010

ACTIVITY

Review

- Identify the cashflow problem that Mr Serepisos' company is experiencing.

- Explain how the global crisis could affect property development businesses such as his.

- By using the term interdependence, explain how the global crisis could impact on the cashflow of Mr Serepisos' companies and his creditors.

- Identify two solutions to Mr Serepisos' cashflow problems.

Research

- Update your knowledge of this case study and find out how Mr Serepisos tried to solve this cashflow problem.

- Identify Mr Serepiso's current financial position.

Senior Business Studies ISBN 9780170215732

Controlling financial information for reporting and decision-making

At the end of this unit you will be able to:

- Use financial information for controlling, reporting and decision-making.
- Explain the need for internal financial controls.

Unit 12 used the example of Manukau's Boardertown to demonstrate the importance of keeping accurate financial records, and to continually monitor current financial performance. We also saw by using the example of Apple how financial success can be represented on the balance sheet and the profit and loss account. Then in Unit 13 we were introduced to their cashflow statement. These documents are presented to stakeholders in the form of published accounts.

Presenting financial information is just one aspect of the accounting function in a business. The functions of internal control and decision-making can also be supported to then make adjustments to operations and ensure that the business aims and objectives remain on track.

In this unit we return to decision-making to examine how financial information can assist business owners. We look at a number of internal control methods that monitor financial performance, such as budgets and variance analysis.

Decision-making as a flow process

As we saw in Unit 11 the decision-making process should be regarded as a flow process, moving from the initial idea or objective to research, then to action, then to review and more research, and on to new ideas and so on.

Financial information allows us to:

- Review a decision to see if it lived up to expectations, in terms of expected sales or customer feedback.
- Identify whether or not mistakes were made.
- Identify what action, if any, needs to be taken next.
- Determine whether or not any adjustments are minor/tactical, or if they involve more significant strategic changes.

Senior Business Studies   ISBN 9780170215732

Measuring performance and suggesting change

Let's return to a well-known fast food business (KFC), which had a successful year in 2011. As we saw in Unit 7 the business created a great deal of publicity with the release of their Double Down burger.

Our new review of the business will consist of three sections:

1 Restaurant Brand's current financial performance.

2 The impact of its decision to release the Double Down burger.

3 A review of a possible strategic move to add a new product to its portfolio of brands in New Zealand. It is a brand that has been very successful in the US.

Part 1: The current financial performance

CASE STUDY

Restaurant Brands lifts full-year profit

Restaurant Brands NZ, the fast food franchise operator, posted a 24% gain in full-year profit as demand at its KFC stores continued to grow.

The Auckland-based company reported a net profit of $24.3 million compared to $19.5 million, a year earlier.

The result was within the firm's forecast $24 million to $26 million range.

The company warned though that the tough external environment would make future gains profit growth difficult.

'Restaurant Brands has demonstrated resilience in the recent tough economic environment, however the current trends mean taking a more cautious approach in looking at the year ahead,' the company said in a statement.

April 2011

ISBN 9780170215732

Senior Business Studies

Discussion

- Explain whether or not you think that KFC had a successful trading year between 2010/11. What other financial and non-financial information would you need before you could make an accurate judgment on the answer?

- By considering the views of KFC's stakeholders, why do you think that the company is warning that 'a tough economic environment means taking a more cautious approach'?

Part 2: The impact of the decision to release the Double Down burger

CASE STUDY >>>

KFC Double Down eats into Pizza Hut's profit

The successful launch of the KFC Double Down in New Zealand ate into the profits of Pizza Hut over the same time, said Restaurant Brands CEO Russell Creedy.

Creedy said KFC sold more than 60,000 of the bun-less chicken burgers.

'This represents a rate that is nearly five times the rate achieved in the United States and Canada during their successful initial Double Down launches.'

'We were particularly pleased with the Double Down sales given this was achieved with minimal marketing expenditure but unprecedented publicity.'

'The success of the Double Down contributed to negative Pizza Hut same store sales figures, which were down 15.7%. That was a concern and action would be taken to rectify this soon,' said Creedy in a further statement.

June 2011

ACTIVITY

Thinking

- Why do you think that Restaurant Brands were unhappy that Pizza Hut profits fell?

- Fully explain whether or not you think the launch of the Double Down burger was successful for Restaurant Brands.

- What action do you think Restaurant Brands could take to increase sales in its Pizza Hut stores?

Part 3: A decision to be made

CASE STUDY

Restaurant Brands eyes Mexican menu after successful launch of the Double Down

Restaurant Brands is still some way from deciding whether to bring Taco Bell to this country, but believes the American chain, which provides Mexican-style food, would have potential here in New Zealand.

Chief executive Russell Creedy told its annual general meeting yesterday no decision had yet been made on whether Restaurant Brands would introduce a fourth brand.

Talks had been held with Taco Bell brand owner Yum! 'Restaurant Brands executives had spent some time visiting Taco Bell in the United States, evaluating its stores and products,' Mr Creedy said.

'We believe that the brand does have an opportunity in New Zealand, but there is a considerable amount of work yet to do before we can make a decision to undertake a pilot in this country.'

June 2011

ISBN 9780170215732

Senior Business Studies

ISBN 9780170215732

Review

- Explain the purpose of an 'annual general meeting' for a large business such as Restaurant Brands.

- Explain how market research could help Restaurant Brands to decide 'if the brand does have an opportunity in New Zealand.'

- Taco Bell has been a success in the US. Why should Restaurant Brands still be careful about using US sales data to forecast New Zealand sales?

Research

- Prepare a questionnaire for use in your class to see how much brand awareness exists around Taco Bell. It should contain 12-15 questions.

- Prepare a brief report to Mr Creedy outlining the possible opportunities and threats to Restaurant Brands of deciding to launch Taco Bell in New Zealand. You could conduct a full SWOT analysis and look at issues around marketing and social responsibility.

The need for internal controls

From the case study above it would appear that Restaurant Brands are going to take some time before they decide to risk launching a new brand in New Zealand, despite the considerable success achieved in the Double Down campaign.

Throughout this study of business we have emphasised the need for innovation, entrepreneurship and risk-taking in order to generate new business start-up ideas. With successful internal and external growth strategies in place, any small SME can then grow into a larger, sustainable business and be a good corporate citizen, providing opportunities for other stakeholders in local and global markets.

These good intentions are jeopardised unless we have controls within a business. We have seen that with the existence of external stakeholders, businesses need to be careful how they manage their public image. The same needs to be said about their internal controls.

Paul Rose, in his book *Organisation and Management*, states the case for internal controls very clearly by using the example of driving a car. The idea of driving provides a very useful way to introduce the need for controls in a business.

'Once we have decided to do something we need to control what we do ... We need to control the speed, direction and plan the most effective route, which saves time and fuel. We need to check the oil, water, and tyre pressure and top up the petrol or diesel.

We must do this before we start and then conduct regular checks as we proceed especially on a long journey. We can do this by checking the instruments on the dashboard as we drive along. We must also check ourselves. Are we tired, do we need a break, are we going on the right road?

The warning lights on the dashboard may tell us about the state of the car but we should also ensure that as managers and leaders we are also healthy and efficient.'

The key areas of control are concerned with:

- Monitoring and maintaining financial performance.

- Monitoring costs of the business by using budgets and variances.

- Monitoring sales revenues to ensure that our forecasts are realistic, and that our future expectations of profit can be fulfilled.

- Monitoring performance of management and workers to ensure that all are working together for the same goals and trying to maximise productivity.

Control as a process

The process of internal control is similar to the decision-making and market research processes. It is typically represented as a circle, because when all steps have been completed they are repeated again and again. It is also known as the PDCA (Plan, Do, Check, Action) cycle:

Plan

Design your control process to find out what is going wrong. Collect data and find out the extent of the problem and create a control plan.

Check

Measure the final results and report back to the key decision-makers.

Do

Carry out the control plan and collect further data.

Action

Modify the process as necessary so that mistakes are not repeated and take whatever action is required.

ISBN 9780170215732

Senior Business Studies

The PDCA Cycle

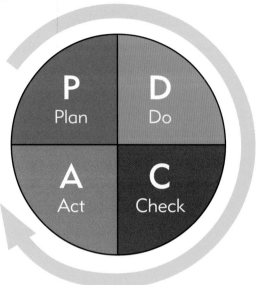

Budgets

Definition

A **budget** is a financial target or prediction of how much a firm is expected to spend or receive in a given time period.

The PDCA cycle forces businesses to constantly review their operations to make sure that they are in control of costs and achieving an appropriate level of revenue.

However, for increased accuracy and control businesses create budgets. Budgets allow businesses to create a performance standard by which they can measure whether they are under or over performing. Put another way, a budget can be used to see if a business is being less or more efficient with the available resources.

Budgets have been described as a route map in helping a business achieve its objectives for a predetermined time period. They can:

- Impose financial control on departments, as the managers of these departments will have to show why they are over or under their budget.

- Provide financial motivation (and thus rewards) to managers who meet and/or exceed targets, especially if McGregor's Theory X (see page 145) approach is being used.

- Allow senior managers to review performance if a decision about new strategy or product development has taken place.

ISBN 9780170215732

Senior Business Studies

Variance analysis

A variance, which can either be positive (favourable) or negative (unfavourable), occurs if the actual figure – perhaps determined by implementing a PDCA cycle – is lower (in the case of costs) or higher (in the case of revenues).

Let us return to the LA Galaxy case study of Unit 11 (pages 78-79). Read Mr Winder's review of what went wrong with the match between LA Galaxy and the Oceania All Stars:

- Primary driver was the loss of $1.79 million.

- Costs of $3,057,602 were $151,052 or 5.2% above the original budget.

- Revenue of $2,075,599 was 61% lower than expected.

- Expected revenue from ticket sales was $2,577,100 but was actually $782,000 (70% less than hoped for).

ACTIVITY

Review

- Use the information above to complete the following table and the activity below.

Item	Budgeted figure	Actual	Variance (all adverse)
Costs		$3,057,602	$151,052
Revenue		$2,075,599	
Expected or forecast revenue		$782,000	

- Having carried out the variance analysis, what action needs to be taken if David Beckham or another famous soccer player is invited to participate in an exhibition match in 2012?

Discussion

- Do you think another match involving a different famous footballer should be organised in 2013? Why or why not? Explain your answer.

ISBN 9780170215732

15 Market research

At the end of this unit you will be able to:

- Describe the importance of market research.
- Design, conduct and present market research for a product.

Level 2 students will need to consider in more detail how firms undertake market research by looking at the role of **sampling** and how we can then present the information to stakeholders.

Definitions

Primary or **field research** is the gathering of first hand or new data that is related to business operations. The most popular way to collect this information is through questionnaires or interviews, although businesses frequently collect data on business products using online surveys. Some businesses invite their stakeholders to give direct feedback in group sessions on company performance, discussing their brand reputation and trialling new products using **focus groups**.

ISBN 9780170215732

Secondary or **desk research** is information collected from sources that have been published by another organisation or government agency, or in publications such as journals, magazines or newspapers, and is freely available from the Internet. The information may not be specific to a businesses needs about its own products, however it can provide extensive information about the external environment.

The importance of market research

In this unit we are going to look at why both small and large businesses carry out market research. We will look at the role of both **primary** and **secondary** research, the costs and benefits of using different types of market research, and how firms can use this information to identify **market segments**.

We can then see how firms use this research to target their existing and potential customers, and use the information to help us define a marketing mix for a business (see Unit 16).

Links to other topic areas

- Level 1: This unit has links to AS 90842 (one-off business activity) and AS 90840 (marketing mix assessment).

- Level 2: This unit links to AS 90846 (design, conduct and present market research for a new or existing product), as well as to AS 90848 (plan, take to market, review and then refine a business activity incorporating a community well-being focus, basing recommendations for the future on market feedback).

The role of ICT in market research

Given the increasing competition and changes in the external environment, some businesses often conduct market research looking for quick and immediate feedback on a new product, advert or promotion. The Internet has allowed businesses to do this with just a few clicks of a mouse. Twitter and Facebook are other ways a business can access feedback on a new product in both local and overseas markets.

ISBN 9780170215732
Senior Business Studies

Sources of market research: primary and secondary

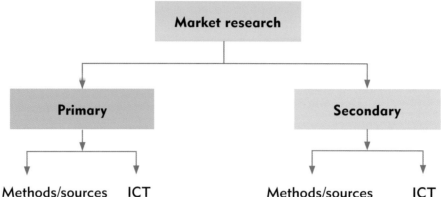

| Market research |
| Primary | Secondary |

Primary

Methods/sources
- Interviews
- Questionnaires
- Surveys
- Focus groups
- Specialist market research agency

ICT
- Data from customer loyalty programmes, such as Flybuys or credit cards
- Surveys

Secondary

Methods/sources
- Internal data from accounts
- Government
- Trade journals
- Magazines
- Surveys
- Newspapers

ICT
- Websites
- Databanks
- Informal (social media networks)

CASE STUDY

Georgie Pie revival hopes kept alive

McDonald's says it may resurrect Georgie Pie, the New Zealand restaurant chain that closed down more than a decade ago. However, an Auckland businessman, who says his own plans to reintroduce the brand were thwarted by McDonald's, reckons the fast food giant sees a return of the pie chain as a threat to burger sales.

McDonald's acquired Georgie Pie, which closed in 1999, from Progressive Enterprises in 1996 and holds the trademark and intellectual property rights. Managing director Mark Hawthorne said the company had been conducting consumer research to find out 'how, when or if' the pie brand could make a 21st century comeback.

'What we do know is there's love for the brand, but part of that love was based on the fact that the pies were [sold for] $1, 15 years ago,' he said. Hawthorne said a Georgie Pie product would need to sell for at least $2.90.

But Martin Gummer, a former North Shore baking company owner who approached McDonald's about rekindling the pie brand in 2008, said he

Senior Business Studies   ISBN 9780170215732

believed the fast-food giant talked about bringing back the brand to dissuade people, like himself, who wanted to have a go at reintroducing it. 'McDonald's realises the pie market in New Zealand is actually a very big market – it's a bigger market than the hamburger market,' Gummer said. 'If you look at it in big picture terms, McDonald's biggest threat is not Burger Fuel or whatever else, it's [a return of] Georgie Pie.'

Hawthorne said the company had invested a lot of money into consumer research around Georgie Pie, which showed it had serious intentions around re-launching the brand. A 'Bring Back Georgie Pie!' Facebook page has more than 45,000 members.

July 2011

ACTIVITY

Review

- What do you think is the best way for McDonald's to find out whether or not they should relaunch the Georgie Pie brand?

- Should McDonald's use primary or secondary data methods to find out the size of the pie market in New Zealand? Explain your answer.

- Georgie Pie was closed down in 1999, explain why you think that primary data would not be as useful for McDonald's to help in its decision-making.

- From the information in the article only, write two reasons for and against McDonald's re-introducing Georgie Pie.

- From the article, explain how important market research will help McDonald's decide the best way to relaunch Georgie Pie in New Zealand.

Evaluation and segmentation

Market research can be very helpful in grouping customers with similar needs and wants together within a whole market. This allows businesses to create market segments that **target** their marketing effort and will eventually lead to the creation of an appropriate marketing mix.

Segmentation of a market can be carried out by:

- Age.
- Gender.
- Cultural or ethnicity.
- Geographical location.
- Lifestyle.
- Occupational background.

ISBN 9780170215732 Senior Business Studies

Before we look more closely at this market research, we need to think about some of the strengths and weaknesses around the collection of primary and secondary data. This normally takes the form of a review of market research data, which helps to see if there needs to be any adjustment in our research process. (This is an important element in AS 90848.) The abbreviation ORCA is useful to help remember the four main points: Objectivity, Relevance, Cost and Accuracy:

 **Objectivity**

- When collecting market research data, your results will be influenced by a variable called bias. It is hard to define exactly, but bias can influence your results to such an extent that the researcher may not end up with any useful information at all. A lack of knowledge, embarrassment, location issues or simply refusing to answer a direct question can lead to bias.

 **Relevance**

- If a company is launching a new product in the marketplace, finding secondary data will be hard, even in overseas markets. Primary data may also be difficult for a new product, unless the consumer taking part has a good idea or a sample of it.

 Cost

- For a small business to start-up, the cost of employing a specialist market research company may be too high. However, it may reduce bias and save considerable time.

- Secondary data collected through the Internet may be cheaper and immediate but …

 **Accuracy**

- … as soon as secondary data is published it is out of date. How accurate will McDonald's information about Georgie Pie be 12 years after the product was discontinued?

Discussion

- Explain the bias in market research results that could arise in the following situations:

  – Asking somebody over the age of 50 years what they think about Minecraft, a new online game.

Senior Business Studies   ISBN 9780170215732

– Asking a vegetarian whether or not Georgie Pie with meat should be relaunched in New Zealand.

– Asking somebody in the street for their age and income level.

– Asking a user of Apple computers on their thoughts of using a PC.

Some businesses are so fearful of introducing bias that they seek the highest degree of objectivity by asking specialist market research companies to collect primary data for them. The following case study highlights this problem of bias.

CASE STUDY

Canterbury fails to catch World Cup fever

Cantabrians, starved of Rugby World Cup games, are struggling to get enthusiastic about the tournament, which kicks off next month.

A new UMR Research poll, which quizzed New Zealanders about the six-week event, found fewer than four in 10 Kiwis are looking forward to the tournament, which will be the largest in this country's sporting history.

The poll found 35% of those surveyed said they were not looking forward to the event, while 37% were looking forward to it. Another 29% were neutral about their views on the World Cup.

Enthusiasm was 'particularly low'' in Canterbury, which was stripped of its five pool matches and two quarterfinals after officials could not guarantee earthquake-damaged AMI Stadium would be ready.

The poll found just 16% of those polled, or about one in six people, said they were keenly anticipating the tournament, 'suggesting they are feeling left out after games were moved away from Christchurch'.

In other poll findings, 51% thought the World Cup would be good for the New Zealand economy, 15% disagreed and 32% had no view either way.

It also revealed 41% of those polled thought the tournament would be disruptive for the country, while just 23% disagreed.

The poll also found 40% believed all the stadium developments around the country would be ready in time, while 14% disagreed.

The online survey polled a representative sample of 850 New Zealanders aged 18 and over.

August 2011

Senior Business Studies   ISBN 9780170215732

ISBN 9780170215732

Review

- Identify and explain the bias which exists in this Christchurch survey about attitudes to the Rugby World Cup 2011.

Discussion

- What measures could the online market research company have carried out to reduce bias in the results?

Research

- Write a questionnaire of 12 questions that would allow you to overcome some of the difficulties present in the above article.

Design, conduct and present market research for a new or existing product

We have carried out a review of the market research methods for two reasons.

Firstly, when designing and conducting market research for a new (or even pre-existing) product, the researcher must anticipate the issues raised by ORCA. Sampling in market research is one way to overcome some of these difficulties.

Secondly, for the Internal Assessment Achievement Standard AS 90848, students have to refine a business plan for their business activity after one cycle of that activity has been carried out. This refinement will include some detailed market research of the first cycle. Unless the students understand and correct weaknesses in their first planning attempt, then important lessons will not have been learned.

The importance of sampling

When designing and conducting a market research survey, choosing the appropriate sample group to ask can improve the accuracy of the research and save valuable time and resources.

If the sample group is based on their geographical location, this type of sampling technique is called **cluster sampling**. If the sample group is based on individuals that have similar characteristics it is called **quota sampling**.

In the LA Galaxy example in Unit 11, it was noted that David Beckham is considered to be very popular particularly with Asian and Pacific peoples. A

Senior Business Studies

market research survey among this group may therefore have given more confidence to the organisers and promoters of the game that the decision to bring the team over was correct.

Of course, these samples will also be biased, since the market survey would be targeting people who already know about David Beckham and LA Galaxy, and who would be more likely to pay to see the team play.

Going beyond the sample group and asking any person outside of the cluster group is known as **random sampling**. It is less prone to bias, but the results may be more variable. Some respondents may have heard of David Beckham, but not LA Galaxy, for instance.

Presenting market research data

Given the widespread availability of software such as Excel or Numbers, which allow students to generate sophisticated diagrams and tables at the touch of a button, the need to explain the different forms of data presentation is omitted here. It is assumed that the student understands how to correctly draw and label a bar chart.

One aspect of presentation not available on a computer, however, involves looking at the reasons behind a particular choice for displaying different types of data, and how these choices impact on the effectiveness of the message. The following exercises review your knowledge in the topic area.

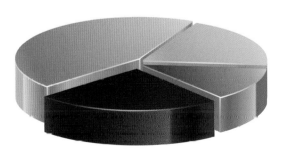

Studying methods of data presentation is no substitute to actually going out 'into the field' and doing it! The experiential approach to the learning of business is a key to gaining control of this subject.

ISBN 9780170215732

Senior Business Studies

Review

- Explain the bias in each of the following situations.

  - Asking an Auckland rugby fan about the strength of Otago in the ITM cup.

  - Asking a pensioner who has no computer about their Facebook page.

  - Asking your friend who owns an iPad about the merits of a Galaxy Tablet.

  In each case, explain how you would use sampling to make your market research more accurate (or reduce bias).

Inquiry

- Define the following terms relating to the presentation of data:

  - Bar chart.

  - Histogram.

  - Pie chart.

  - Pictogram.

- Explain why bar charts are useful in presenting data.

- Explain two problems when using a pie chart to present data.

- Imagine you are given a set of data. You need to decide how you would best present the data, bearing in mind the appropriateness of the presentation method and how to make your chosen method the most effective to the reader.

  - The sales figures for a soft drink company over the last ten years.

  - Data to show the number of industrial accidents and injuries in large business over the past two years.

  - The male/female ratio in your current class.

  - The numbers of different nationalities present in your school.

  - The income/wage levels of ten different occupations.

ACTIVITY

- A senior manager in a music store is looking at the sales figures of three music departments. She is trying to decide which department is doing the 'best.' Assume that the current external environment has affected all three departments in the same way. The senior manager cannot tell who is doing the best: the Jazz supervisor says that his department has had the biggest increase in sales; the NZ Rock supervisor argues that her department still contributes the most to sales; the Alternative supervisor argues that since his range was only released last year, his department has had the largest percentage increase in sales. Advise the senior manager as to who you think is doing the 'best'. What does this activity reveal about the difficulties in interpreting sales data accurately? How do we decide who or what is really doing the 'best'?

Year	2010	2011	2012
Jazz	1.2	1.8	2.0
NZ Rock	2.0	2.4	2.1
Alternative	0.2	0.4	0.8
Total	3.4	4.6	4.9

(Figures for music sales in million of dollars)

Research

- Before you begin your internal assignment for either Level 1 or 2, it would be a good idea to conduct a small survey of your class around a topic. Some survey ideas are given below. Write up your results and try to identify ways in which your market research approach could have been improved.

  - A survey of mobile phone use in terms of minutes/hours spent texting.

  - A survey to find who is using which mobile phone provider in New Zealand.

  - A survey of the most popular websites in your class and Internet surfing habits such as time spent per day etc.

Senior Business Studies ISBN 9780170215732

The marketing mix

The problem

Imagine that you are passionate and really confident about the commercial success of your new product or service in the marketplace. You undertake considerable market research and identify a suitable target market. You invest in creating a small batch of samples, price the product lower than the competition, and conduct a marketing campaign on Facebook or another social networking site (as this is effectively free) and have it ready to be sold direct from your own home.

But not one purchase is made ...

Remember the open air cinema example from Unit 2?

- Even if you carry out extensive market research, it is no guarantee of sales.

The solution

Market research is very important but if your business is to be effective the research must be translated into an **effective marketing mix to suit your target market**.

Definition

Marketing: The process of identifying and satisfying consumer wants and needs in line with the objectives of the business.

ISBN 9780170215732

Senior Business Studies

The basic marketing mix

These are the elements or variables that form the basis of a marketing plan. They are known as the 4 P's. Only a brief outline is given here as it is expected that many students will either google the market mix or already be familiar with this term and what it means.

 ## Product

- What is the product to be sold to the customer?

- Who is the intended market?

- How is the product going to be different from competitors in the marketplace?

 ## Price

- Which pricing method will we use?

- What pricing method will be the most appropriate to meet the needs of the target market?

- How will the pricing method affect the image of the product?

 ## Place (or how the product will be distributed to the end user)

- Will the business use retail shops?

- Will the product be sold online directly to the customer?

- How will the business deal with customers in other countries?

 ## Promotion (including advertising, branding, packaging and other selling strategies)

- What is the most effective way to get the product noticed in a competitive market?

- Should the business use viral marketing and the Internet to create stakeholder interest?

- Will the business need to be controversial to get consumer attention?

- How much will need to be spent on (the range of) promotional activities?

The marketing mix in relation to the target market

Each company has a unique marketing mix for its particular product or service. If marketing mixes were identical between businesses then stakeholders could become confused, consumer choice would narrow. Potential profits would be more difficult to achieve as a result.

ISBN 9780170215732

Senior Business Studies

Successful domestic and global businesses now constantly review their marketing effort to ensure that consumers continue to be satisfied. In order to do this they ask themselves a number of important questions about their mix, including but not limited to:

- How good is our product? Do we need to modify or change it?

- Are we charging the right price? The Internet now has made pricing more difficult due to 'transparency'. It is much easier now for your competitors to see your prices using sites such as www.pricespy.co.nz (see the case study on pricing a new 2011 Rugby World Cup jersey).

- Is our promotional mix correct and are we reaching the right target market?

- What is the best way for our products to reach the consumer? Should we be worried about the global trend in online retailing and close some of our retail outlets?

We will consider the marketing mix more generally by looking at a few New Zealand examples. Read through the case studies below, use the Internet to undertake secondary research to fill in any gaps in your knowledge, and complete the activities that follow.

Backwards lurch to leap forward

One of New Zealand's oldest and best-known brands is getting a facelift.

On February 27, a $1.25 million marketing campaign featuring a new 'retro' label for soft-drink L&P will launch. Bottles with the new label will be in stores from May – elbowing aside those wearing the familiar yellow wrap-around that has sported L&P in fat white letters since the mid-1980s.

The slogan 'World famous in New Zealand' is being altered: the phrase 'since ages ago' will be tacked on at the end.

The senior brand manager for L&P owner Coca-Cola Amatil NZ, Megan Denize, said the campaign had been designed to remind Kiwis that New Zealand was a great place in which to grow up. 'While New Zealand has a multitude of traditional kiwiana treasures – including gumboots, Buzzy Bees, pavlova and Swandris - there's a younger generation of L&P drinkers who relate to a different and more recent range of icons.'

Can a 'bring back the mullet' competition and commercials featuring stubbies and Speedos put more fizz into L&P? Or could change put growth of

L&P sales at risk given that some may argue that the marketing is 'old fashioned.'

Brand strategist Brian Richards, the man behind the Cervena campaign for New Zealand venison, believes the choice of 1970s and 1980s images is 'ill-advised' and old fashioned.

But other brand experts thought it was the right decision. 'It's the right thing to do,' said Howard Russell, head of branding consultancy Strategic Insight. 'This is presumably an attempt to de-Coke and de-Fanta it ... they're obviously trying to inject a more potent personality [into L&P].'

He said Bundaberg ginger beer had had success with the same type of marketing, pitching itself as old fashioned – but also a product with genuine character.

Sarena Longley, a lecturer at Victoria University's school of marketing did not believe the revamp was a major risk.

L&P senior brand manager Megan Denize said there were several reasons for the rebranding. 'The soft drink market segment is saturated with brands that are trying to be cool and contemporary that there is little point trying to modernise L&P,' she said. 'We believe we can achieve effective marketing by doing completely the opposite.'

The campaign would target 16-year-olds to 29-year-olds who may be less familiar with the brand's status

The slogan had stayed (with the addition) because 'it is so closely associated with L&P that we would be mad to change it.'

The three-month gap between the start of the campaign and the introduction of the bottle in stores was intended to minimise the most significant risk the company could see – that consumers might not recognise the bottle.

Many older consumers bought L&P because they remembered drinking it as children and the change had to reinforce the sense of New Zealand heritage among younger drinkers.

'What we needed to do was move the brand forward – or in this case, backward,' said Denize.

February 2005

CASE STUDY ▷▷▷

Pizzas go to hell and back

When Hell Pizza opened up above the old Victoria University squash club in Wellington, it seemed like a mad idea.

One tiny kitchen, three guys with caffeine-shot eyes, pizza named after the seven deadly sins. Craziest of all, selling expensive but quality pizzas to poor students.

ISBN 9780170215732

Senior Business Studies

Hell has grown by combining controversial marketing and hard work with a really good product.

Then they sold their souls to big business. In 2006, for about $15 million, Burger King franchisee Tasman Pacific Foods Group acquired the pizza chain, while the boys set off to open up shop in Australia, Britain and Ireland.

Back home, Hell still kept the Advertising Standards Authority busy with complaints about a condom giveaway promoting its 'Lust' pizza, offensive billboards and low cost viral marketing ideas through You Tube clips.

But mistakes were made. A leaked memo told owners to cut toppings by a quarter, while maintaining prices and secrecy. The new owners had forgotten that while branding was important, quality was critical and the competitive weapon in a market with many competitors.

This week, the Hell boys bought back their company. The brand had got confused, they said. They would target quality, rather than trying to compete on price with Domino's.

It is a timely reminder that Brand NZ is founded on excellence, not gimmicks. And now, the Hell boys are firmly on the side of the angels.

May 2009

ACTIVITY

Review

- What is the 4 P marketing mix of L&P and Hell Pizza?

- Identify any similarities or differences between the marketing conducted by both companies.

- What is viral marketing? Why do you think a company such as Hell Pizza uses viral marketing?

- Explain the importance of the 'product' in the marketing mix of both companies.

Discussion

- L&P's approach is to use a traditional or retro styling to their labeling and product. Explain whether you think this will be more effective among (a) the 18-30 market segment, or (b) the over 50 market segment.

Research

- What are the 7 P's?

- Why do we need an additonal 3 P's?

The production process and supply chain

17

At the end of this unit you will be able to:

- Describe the production process of goods and/or services.

- Explain factors in relation to the production process and the supply chain.

With more industries now becoming competitive, and markets becoming saturated, businesses are looking closely at ways to produce more efficiently so as to cut costs and boost profits. The way in which products are produced – called the **production process** – has come under increasing scrutiny.

In this unit we will introduce a number of new business terms for Level 1, and then look at the **supply chain process** in greater detail for Level 2 students, linking to **outsourcing** as a way of achieving **economies of scale**.

Definitions

The **production process** is a way to organise resources to meet a customer need or want. In a manufacturing business, production is the whole process; obtaining raw materials, processing them into finished products, and delivering to the final customer. The term production process can also be applied to the delivery of services.

Economies of scale occur when doubling the amount of raw materials in the production process leads to a much larger increase in outputs (i.e. more than double). Under these conditions, the cost per unit of output produced will fall. This fundamental concept used in economics will be introduced to help students understand when some types of production process are more appropriate to produce certain goods and services to others. (See also the units on growth strategies and globalisation.)

Senior Business Studies   ISBN 9780170215732

Job, batch and flow production methods

The table below outlines the differences between production methods and provides a few examples of each.

Production method	Description	Examples	
Job	The production process is tailored around making one-off items specific to customer needs or industry requirements.	A hand-made suit or a wedding cake for consumers. A bridge construction or special effects on a particular film.	
Batch	Items are produced in groups or 'batches' as part of the production process. Each group moves through the process in stages and is not allowed to move on to the next one until the previous step has been completed.	Carefully controlled production process, which allows slight modifications to individual groups. The production of bread, beer and baked beans where some product differences are included.	
Flow	A continuous process. Similar to batch but the group moves from one stage to the next without stopping.	The production of cars provides the classic example of flow production. (Note, however, that luxury cars such as Ferrari and Rolls Royce are produced according to the job production method.)	

Which production process?

Job production lends itself to very small market segments, as the number of items produced is usually very small. For instance, a consumer is usually going to order one wedding cake although it will normally be customised to their individual needs.

Batch production allows for some customisation of products too, for example wholemeal vs wheatmeal vs multigrain bread, or low alcohol/lite vs regular beer.

Flow production is normally used in long production runs, when the potential for economies of scale is considerably higher.

Consider the following case study and answer the questions that follow.

Senior Business Studies   ISBN 9780170215732

CASE STUDY ≫≫≫

'Green' coffee will give the capital quite a kick

Lower Hutt's Celcius Coffee says its next move will be to brew up an appetite for its premium coffee blends in the capital, after firmly establishing its green credentials.

Nick and Stephanie Fry, the husband-and-wife team at the helm of the coffee roasting company, won 'Green Gold' a business Gold Awards in Wellington for its environmentally sustainable practices.

The pair have analysed each stage of the coffee production process and have reduced carbon dioxide emissions wherever they can – including in packaging and purchasing decisions, and offset those emissions they cannot reduce by buying carbon credits.

The company converts unwanted coffee grounds into its Sweet Grounds 'soil conditioner', and has developed the IdealCup, a reusable takeaway coffee cup.

Mr Fry says its coffee is sold in Wellington Foodstuffs supermarkets, Commonsense Organics, through business supplies company Office Max, and in cafes from Lake Tekapo in the South Island to Whitianga up north.

The company's adherence to premium, organic, Fair Trade-licensed beans and environmentally sustainable practice mean Celcius Coffee is among the most expensive at supermarkets, but shoppers are prepared to pay.

January 2005

ACTIVITY

Review

- Identify two objectives of Celcius Coffee.

- Explain the importance for a smaller coffee roaster such as Celcius to be viewed by its stakeholders as environmentally sustainable.

- Identify the most appropriate production process to produce premium coffee.

- Given your answer above suggest an appropriate production process if Celcius wishes to grow its market share and maintain an environmentally sustainable reputation with its stakeholders.

Research

- Look at the different types of economies of scale on offer and the case studies on Branco's Sausages (page 69) and Tasty Pots (page 54). Why do you think these companies continue making most of their products by hand and not use machinery, which could increase output and reduce costs?

Senior Business Studies   ISBN 9780170215732

The supply chain

'The supply chain is no longer a back-office activity. It has become the competitive weapon in the boardroom.'

(Kevin O'Connell, former CEO of IBM, 2005)

Definition

The **supply chain** represents the entire sequence of activities required to turn raw materials into a finished consumer purchase. The chain will include primary, secondary and tertiary activities. A supply chain can also be referred to as the 'logistics process'.

Factors influencing the supply chain

Some very small businesses will have a direct link between themselves and the final customer. This could be described as a short supply chain. They may only use a couple of suppliers and may transport the finished product to the customer themselves as part of their customer service. They may operate in local markets only.

Large businesses however, may have a number of supplier, retailer and customer relationships spread throughout the world as part of their supply chain. One large supermarket in the UK, Tesco, has leased its own fleet of aircraft to transport products from around the world to take advantage of the differences in cost of the global market place.

A diagram of possible supply chain links is given below.

Supply chain links

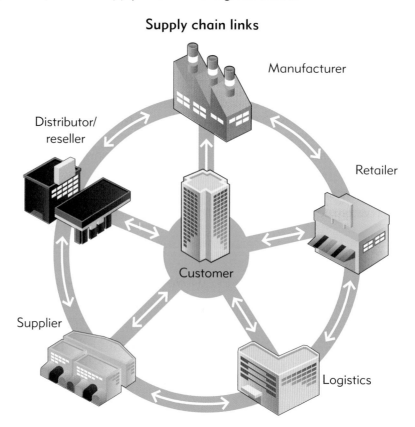

ISBN 9780170215732

Senior Business Studies

We can summarise that some of the key factors influencing the supply chain. These factors are linked closely to the reasons why some large businesses wish to vertically integrate as we shall see in the next unit.

- A company such as Apple may have their research facilities in the United States, the manufacturing carried out in China and their retailing operations dispersed throughout the world using local agents or large retail chains acting as 'resellers' to provide their products to the final consumer

- The size and geographical spread of the market the firm is wishing to sell into.

- The degree of control the firm wishes to exert over the whole supply chain. If a business wishes to have total control due to quality concerns, it may be reluctant to let other firms supply it with components or give them raw materials or even offer the finished product to customers.

- The availability of reliable and cheap communication media between suppliers, customers and retailers.

- The extent to which their competitors are using other countries or firms as part of their supply chain may force large businesses to undertake a process known as Outsourcing or Offshoring.

Supply chain for beer production

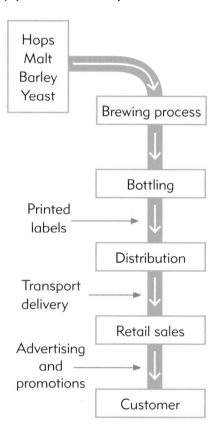

Definitions

Outsourcing is a process in which business will subcontract or use independent suppliers rather than undertake the activities themselves.

Offshoring is a term used when these subcontracted activities occur outside the country of origin (from our perspective, outside of New Zealand).

Outsourcing

As we shall see in Unit 24, many large New Zealand businesses such as Masport, Orca and MacPac have decided to outsource parts of their supply chain to other countries.

Mostly, these businesses have outsourced the manufacturing parts of the supply chain to countries with lower wages than New Zealand, considerably reducing production costs and with no loss of finished product quality.

Understandably, stakeholders affected by these changes have been concerned, especially when the cost savings from outsourcing are not been passed on in lower prices to the consumer.

Senior Business Studies   ISBN 9780170215732

All Black jersey makers paying some workers 60c per hour – Oxfam

Adidas is trying to block cheap imports of the new All Blacks jersey to New Zealand and is paying the people who make their products as little as 60c an hour.

Non-profit organisations such as Oxfam have highlighted the fact that many factories used by Adidas in their supply chain pay their workers poor wages while making huge profits.

Oxfam, Play Fair and China Labor Watch say wages at Adidas factories in Asia are as low as 60c an hour.

The Rugby World Cup-branded jerseys are made in Thailand, and the non-tournament All Blacks jerseys are made in China, where Adidas has come under scrutiny for poor wages.

Adidas's response last year to concerns about low wages at its factory in Indonesia was that the company promoted 'improved wage-setting mechanisms' to ensure fair payment. It also noted that it was providing employment in poverty stricken countries.

Oxfam New Zealand executive director Barry Coates said wages had remained at the bare minimum, although the worst abuses in sporting brands' sweatshop had waned in recent years because of publicity. 'It seems rather obscene that all of the value is being captured by the rugby union and Adidas and none of the value is being captured by the workers who are at minimum wage or close to it,' Mr Coates said.

'That's not fair. The fair way to do it is to share the value up the supply chain because people can understand that if you can sell things for higher prices, then surely people who make them should have a share of the higher price.'

August 2011

ACTIVITY

Thinking

- Identify three countries in the Adidas supply chain.
- Identify two stakeholder disagreements in the case study.
- Explain why Adidas have outsourced the production of rugby jerseys to those countries identified above.
- Fully explain whether or not you think that Adidas is being 'ethical' by outsourcing parts of its supply chain to these countries.

Growth strategies

18

At the end of this unit you will be able to:

- Identify different growth strategies and discuss their advantages and disadvantages.

Why grow?

Business textbooks generally assume that all firms should try to grow. There are a number of reasons for this.

- A much larger organisation, with greater financial resources, can grow to protect itself against adverse changes in the external environment.

- With more financial resources, larger firms can take more risks. These are called risk-bearing economies of scale.

- Larger firms can conduct market research and develop new products in new markets, or perhaps look at marketing existing products in new overseas markets. The potential for higher profits is considerable.

- Growth may provide greater security (by purchasing more fixed assets), but also encourage new investors to provide additional capital thereby allowing more funds to be transferred to enterprising or innovative projects.

Economies of scale

Most large or growing businesses can experience considerable cost savings if they look at taking advantage of large-scale production via the supply chain or outsourcing elements of the production process.

ISBN 9780170215732 Senior Business Studies

Types of economies of scale include:

- **Financial**
  Cheaper finance costs through increased confidence on the part of the lender, reducing the interest rate charged.

- **Purchasing**
  Bulk buying of raw materials or finished products. Imagine comparing the per unit cost of a tin of baked beans from Pak N' Save (who might buy 50,000 per week) to that of a local dairy (who may only purchase 25).

- **Marketing**
  Large businesses can advertise on media with huge audience reach, such as prime time TV slots during *Shortland Street* or live sporting events.

- **External**
  Economies of scale can be earned when a whole industry grows. Weta Workshop in Wellington, for instance, have been superb ambassadors for the New Zealand film and special effects industries, and have encouraged a whole new group of film-makers and technicians to train and develop their skills. Ultimately this move leads to reduced labour costs for Weta Workshop and other stakeholders within the local film industry.

Similarly, as the New Zealand wine industry has grown, individual wineries can share research facilities and marketing opportunities, reducing the overall costs of advertising and taking their wines into global markets.

Joint ventures, such as the Green Shell Mussel project between Sanford and Sealord, has allowed a new market opportunity to be developed in China, where an individual firm would find it too expensive to compete alone. Costs of entry into large international markets can be reduced.

Problems with growth

- The market in which the business operates may not be large enough to sustain greater production, leading to waste and losses.

- Product perception in the market could change. The waiting time for a new Ferrari (rumoured to be over two years) only adds to the value of the product, and the company could 'cheapen' their brand by producing more cars for a wider market segment.

- In order to finance growth a firm may have to attract new investors or obtain other sources of finance, which could mean giving up some overall control of the business. In Unit 9 we saw that the Poznanovich family wanted to keep the business under the control of the family and were reluctant to bring in outside capital.

- A larger business can become harder to control and manage effectively. Additional layers of hierarchy may need to be created. Spans of control may widen. Quality control problems for the finished product may emerge, ultimately raising costs per unit.

Senior Business Studies   ISBN 9780170215732

- Communication (see Unit 21) becomes more difficult with longer chains of command. Face to face communication can be replaced with ICT methods such as email, however, worker confusion (and, potentially, isolation) may result. Quality concerns around the finished product could develop.

- The growth of the company may have an impact on its organisational culture (see Unit 23). A business with a flat hierarchy and 'open' culture may be forced to become taller and more autocratic, leading to a negative impact on motivation and changes to the channels of communication.

In the last three points above, difficulties in managing a larger growing business will inevitably lead to increased costs of production, giving rise to a phenomenon known as **diseconomies of scale**. We will look at this point in further detail as we consider the growth strategy of mergers and takeovers more closely.

Growth strategies in more detail

We will look at three different methods of growth both **internal** and **external**:

1 Competition or joint venture.

2 Franchising.

3 Acquisition: Mergers and takeovers.

Growth strategy 1: Expanding production in the current market or increase market share by joint venture

Large businesses could seek growth by trying to charge lower prices than their competitors, to increase sales revenues and volumes and (hopefully) experience economies of scale to boost profits. They could also try to launch new services in the existing market to generate more market share.

Internal growth takes time, so unless the firm decides to move into a new market with it products the opportunities for growth may be limited. There will also need to be extensive (and expensive) market research carried out.

The risks of growing (and consequently spending large sums of money financing this type of expansion) means that some large businesses form joint ventures, agreements or strategic alliances with their rivals, mainly to share costs and equipment but also to reduce risk. Here is one example

ISBN 9780170215732

Senior Business Studies

Qantas set to axe 1000 jobs and introduce new services to boost growth

Qantas is making changes in a bid to boost profitability, a move that will affect about 1000 jobs.

Qantas Airways will make dramatic changes to its international business to make it profitable in a process that will affect 1000 jobs.

'We have established a five-year plan that has the objective, first, of returning Qantas International to profitability in the short term.'

At the end of the process, Qantas would participate in regional Asian opportunities and in the world leading to higher growth than that generated by operating only in the Australian market.

Through a new strategy, Qantas says it will better connect to global cities with new alliance partners. It will:

- Launch a direct flight to Santiago, replacing Buenos Aires as the entry point to South America.
- Consider reviewing its joint agreements with British Airways, American and Malaysia Airlines.

Qantas will also invest in new products and services by:

- Creating a new premium airline based in Asia, with a new name, new aircraft and new look.
- Launching Jet Star Japan as a new low-cost carrier together with Japan Airlines and Mitsubishi.
- Buying up to 110 Airbus A320s to support growth.

August 2011

Qantas' decision to form joint ventures with its competitors is an idea designed to reduce risk and financial commitment to boost growth. Of course any profits and decisions between the two parties will need to be shared. However, by working alongside an existing company Qantas may be able to gain knowledge and benefit from that company's experience of the local market, hence their market research costs will be reduced.

Senior Business Studies   ISBN 9780170215732

Asia is clearly a growing and important market for Australasian businesses. China in particular has been growing at superlative rates, and a number of New Zealand companies are trying to expand by opting to set up a market position in cities such as Beijing and Shanghai.

One excellent example of a joint venture is the Green Shell Mussel project between Sealord, Sanford and the North Island Mussel Processors Ltd (NIMPL). Individually these firms would not have the resources to enter the Chinese market but together they have created a joint venture, which will create an opportunity to increase sales volumes in an overseas market.

Creating new jobs in the process will benefit local communities and ensure their economic sustainability. This type of approach is a model that other large businesses looking for growth in New Zealand would do well to emulate.

Growth strategy 2: Franchising

The benefits to a business of reducing overall risk and level of financial commitment, while simultaneously growing the business, is a strategy that has lead to New Zealand having one of the most franchised business structures in the world.

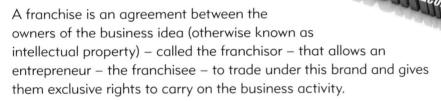

A franchise is an agreement between the owners of the business idea (otherwise known as intellectual property) – called the franchisor – that allows an entrepreneur – the franchisee – to trade under this brand and gives them exclusive rights to carry on the business activity.

Normally the franchisor receives a royalty payment and growth of their idea and a share in future profits, and the franchisee receives training and equipment and commits to ensuring that minimum standards of service are met.

The franchisee benefits by having a large organisation behind them to pay for large advertising expenses and provide a marketing strategy. It also supplies them with a business idea that has proven to be a commercial success in the marketplace. Of course the entrepreneur does give up control to an extent, but since the threat of liability is such an issue for sole traders, some New Zealand entrepreneurs choose to protect themselves by working with an already established business, and especially with well-known household brands.

Growth strategy 3: Acquisition

For very large businesses with vast reserves of cash, the temptation to spend is strong since this usually re-assures its shareholders that the business is using its finances to plan responsibly for future growth. Many large businesses feature growth as part of their mission statements.

Acquisition

The act of acquiring purchase of a company by strategy of buying and selli "friendly" one or a "hostile" merger or takeover accord

ISBN 9780170215732

Senior Business Studies

In rapidly changing markets, however, there may not be time to invest in developing a new business idea. Instead the large business may decide to merge with or take over another company. This is called external growth via acquisition.

Although a number of writers use the terms mergers and take overs to mean the same thing, they are in fact slightly different.

- A merger is defined when two or more companies agree to joining together and move forward as a single new company rather than remain separately owned and operated.

- A takeover is defined as an 'involuntary' merger. One company (X) captures another (Y) and establishes itself as the new owner. This capture is called an acquisition. From a legal view point, company Y ceases to exist.

Types of mergers and takeover

- **Horizontal**
  When two or more firms in the same industry and that produce similar goods and services decide to join together.

- **Vertical**
  When a large firm takes over a firm in its supply chain (see previous unit), so as to guarantee the supply of raw materials or to control more of the retail distribution network. In the former case this is called backwards or upstream vertical integration. In the latter case this is called forwards or downstream integration.

- **Conglomerate**
  When a large firm decides to take over a firm with no link to their current market, goods or services. This strategy is the most risky, and evidence from many conglomerate mergers of the past has shown that bringing together two management teams with different organisational cultures (see Unit 23) can lead to significant diseconomies of scale and losses instead of profits.

The question of intellectual property

Having looked at the different types of mergers, one may question why a large business would wish to acquire another firm in a completely different industry, given the evidence that shows the gains from the takeover are usually outweighed by the losses.

External growth is a quicker way to secure new intellectual property, meaning business ideas that have already been financed and developed by somebody else. Given the need to be sustainable, a number of high profile takeovers have involved larger businesses merging with smaller sustainable businesses, including:

- L'Oreal buying up The Body Shop.

- Cadbury buying organic Fair Trade chocolate producer Green & Black's.

ISBN 9780170215732

- Mass-market juice maker Charlie's purchasing beverage company Phoenix Organic.

On the other hand, a large business may just wish to buy another company to be part of a great business idea!

Read the case study below and answer the questions that follow.

CASE STUDY

Microsoft buys Skype for $US8.5b

Microsoft has announced plans to buy Internet phone service company Skype for US$8.5 billion in a move aimed at carving out a bigger presence in an online arena dominated by Google and Facebook.

The acquisition of Skype, which had reportedly also attracted interest from Cisco, Facebook and Google, is the largest ever by the US software giant.

'Skype is a phenomenal service that is loved by millions of people around the world,' Microsoft chief executive Steve Ballmer said in a statement on Tuesday announcing the purchase.

Tens of millions of people use Skype to make low-cost or free phone calls over the Internet using their computers or smartphones. Skype bypasses the standard telephone network by channeling voice and video calls over the web.

Skype was founded in 2003 and was taken over by online auction giant eBay in September 2005. It was sold to the investment group led by Silver Lake in November 2009 in a deal that valued the company at US$2.75 billion.

Skype has 170 million users and logged more than 207 billion minutes of voice and video conversations in 2010.

Buying Skype could be a way for Microsoft to shed some of its business software image and gain a foothold in a hot smartphone market at a time when Internet lifestyles are going mobile.

Microsoft's Windows is the dominant computer operating system but its Bing search engine lags far behind Google and its Windows Phone mobile platform has been losing market share to Apple's iPhone, Google's Android and Research In Motion's Blackberry.

Magnus Rehle, a business analyst said Microsoft is 'buying a brand and a big chunk of customers.'

'It could (also) be a defensive strategy from them ... to block Facebook and Google from doing it instead,' Rehle added. 'Skype may be a cheap ticket to the next huge search market,' he said.

May 2011

ISBN 9780170215732

Senior Business Studies

ACTIVITY

Review

- Explain why Microsoft bought Skype and identify the type of acquisition.

- What do you think could be the reaction of Google and Facebook to Microsoft's decision?

- How would you measure the benefits of this aquisition and judge that it had been a success?

Research

- The above case study was written in May 2011. Has the acquisition of Skype generated the future benefits Microsoft was hoping for?

- Find out what a franchise agreement looks like by investigating successful franchises such as Subway, McDonalds, Hire a Hubby, Robert Harris, Esquires, Brumby's or Dunk 'N Donuts.

- Compare capital requirements to start up the franchise, and royalty payments.

- Explain why some entrepreneurs choose to purchase a franchise rather than set up their own business.

- Identify three problems in creating a franchise model to generate growth of your business idea.

- Explain the reasons behind Bacardi's takeover of New Zealand alcohol brand 42Below.

Organisational structure

19

At the end of this unit you will be able to:

- Explain business terms related to organisation structure.

- Discuss the types of different business organisational structures and their features.

Although this section is intended for Level 2 study, it is very broad topic and includes references to leadership, motivation and organisational culture, which are covered in other units. It also has links to communication (see Unit 21). Students new to the course are advised to read this unit. The language contains a number of business terms and phrases that may be unfamiliar, making this unit seem 'jargon heavy'. Students will need to regularly check their understanding of key terms.

Definitions

Organisational structure: The way the management of an organisation is arranged in a business. This can be carried out horizontally (by layers of hierarchy) or vertically (by function, operation or matrix).

Authority: Refers to any manager who is given the responsibility to control certain departments or units within a business.

Span of control: The number of workers or subordinates who are under the control of a supervisor or unit manager.

Levels of hierarchy: The number of levels or layers of formal authority within an organisation.

Organisational chart: A diagram showing the lines of authority and layers of hierarchy within an organisation.

ISBN 9780170215732

Senior Business Studies

The choice of **organisational structure** will impact heavily on the final decision as to which legal identity the company chooses to adopt.

The **chain of command** influences how managers and subordinates are expected to communicate within an organisation. It is a vertical line of authority that enables orders to be passed down through the **layers of hierarchy**.

To be effective and useful the chain of command needs to be clear, with each member of the organisational structure being able to see who they need to report to (this is called being **responsible** to).

Some organisations are considered **tall**, with many levels and each manager having a small span of control.

A **flat hierarchy** is an organisational structure with a much larger span of control and fewer levels of hierarchy.

Whether an organisation is tall or flat will largely depend on the **organisational culture**, the number of employees or departments and the leadership style adopted.

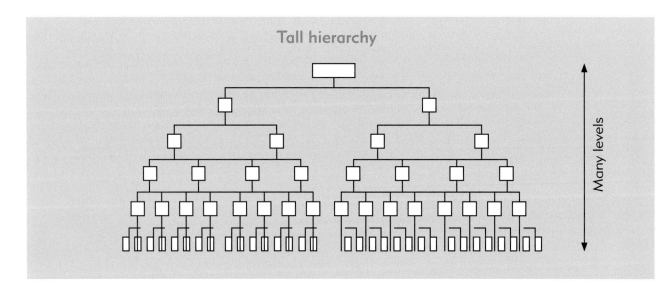

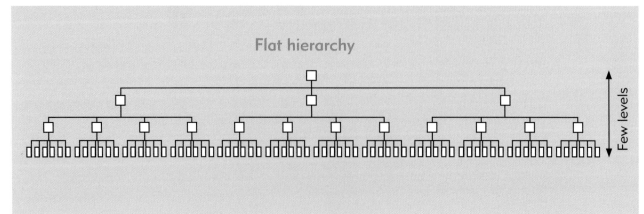

ISBN 9780170215732

Senior Business Studies

Here are some other examples of organisational charts.

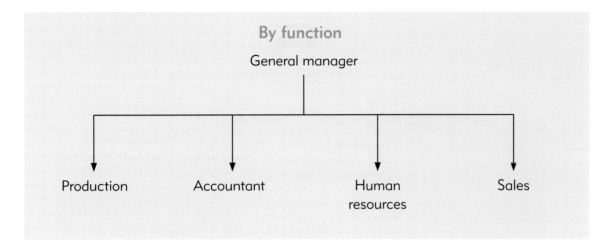

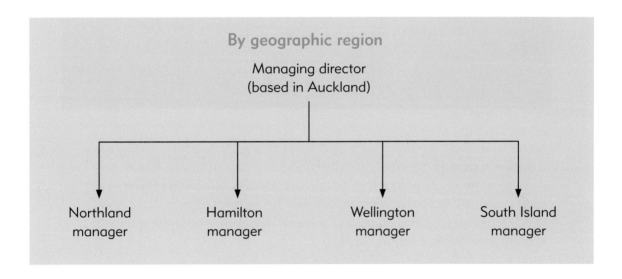

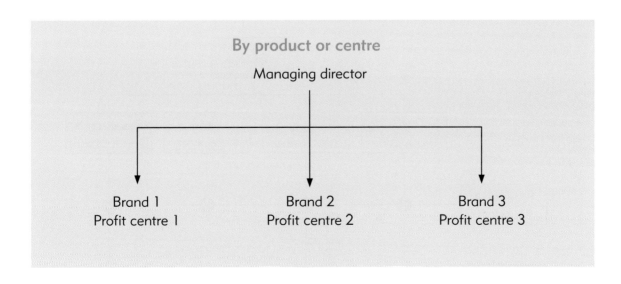

ISBN 9780170215732

Senior Business Studies

Look at the following structure diagram for Sanford Limited.

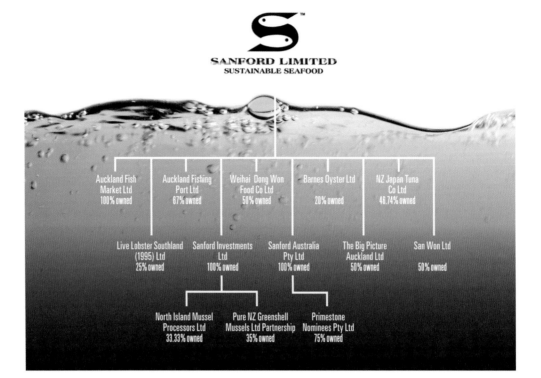

Some businesses are organised using a matrix structure, which occurs when a business creates a project team by taking one person from a functional department such as production, finance, marketing or human resources to produce a 'cell' of four workers responsible for working together on a specific task. Once the project is completed the cell 'disbands' and its members go back to their original departments.

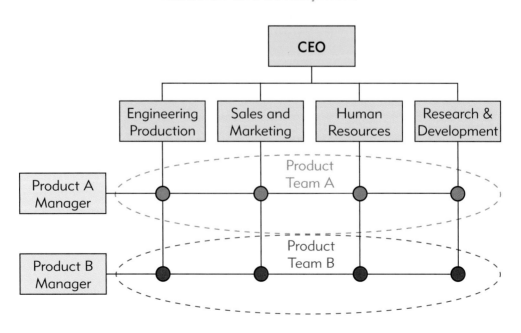

Senior Business Studies   ISBN 9780170215732

ACTIVITY

Inquiry

- Working alone or in pairs, draw the organisational structure of your school or college.

  - Avoid specific names and personalities and focus on roles or job titles.

  - Try not to Google the answer!

- Compare your results with at least three other groups.

  - Are the diagrams similar? What are the differences?

  - If you are all from the same school, why are there differences?

  - Who is at the top and bottom of the organisational chart? Explain why.

- Show your diagram to another stakeholder (such as a parent or former student of the college who may have had an association with the institution in the past).

  - Are there any changes in structure? Has the college's hierarchy become taller or flatter?

  - If the school has grown in size (as expected), have the spans of control become wider?

Discussion

- What are the benefits for stakeholders of drawing a clear organisational chart?

- Explain the benefits to your school or college from having a clear organisational structure.

Research

- Use the Internet to find other examples of organisational structure of New Zealand businesses.

Advantages and disadvantages of different organisational structure

Structure	Advantages	Disadvantages
By function	Clear lines of communication and responsibility. Useful for new employees to see how their new workplace is structured. Encourages specialisation leading to efficiency.	This type of structure may encourage departments to view themselves as isolated and set their own goals or objectives. Relies heavily on the ability of the overall CEO to communicate effectively with all departments.
By geographic location	Allow local managers to make decisions depending on the region. By being close to local markets, the business is able to receive updated research and customer feedback.	Given geographical location or time differences, there is a potential loss of control of objectives by head office. Although with new technologies such as Skype this may not be so much of an issue. Cultural and language issues will need to be considered to smooth communication.
By brand or product	Allows expertise in specific products and markets. Quicker decision-making and easier to measure performance as sales per product easier to identify.	Conflict and competition between brands or products. Product or brand objectives to boost performance rather than applying overall organisation objectives.
Matrix	Allows teams to work together. Form different departments to problem solve. Increasing motivation of its members.	Clear lines of authority need to be established. Who is the boss of the team? After the team breaks up, the relationships and productivity may be lost unless a future problem solving opportunity is given.

What is the most appropriate organisational structure?

Choosing the best organisational structure will depend on a number of factors, the most important being the business objectives of the owners. **The most appropriate structure will allow an organisation to achieve its mission and vision.**

Senior Business Studies   ISBN 9780170215732

Other crucial questions to consider include:

- Does the business wish to expand into new markets?

- Does the leadership want to adopt an open or individualistic culture?

- Is the objective of the business to monitor and control costs and allow no room for discussion of its values and beliefs?

- Does the business wish to split departments in such a way to encourage competition and thus motivate managers towards achieving certain targets around profits or productivity?

- Given growing awareness of the importance of the supply chain and globalisation, does the firm wish to 'de-layer' and allow certain parts of its production process to be carried out by a manufacturer in other countries? (See also Unit 17 pages 121-122.)

Organisational restructuring

Businesses rarely stand still, however, and shareholders and owners are constantly looking for ways to improve efficiency, increase motivation and generate additional profitability. One way for a large business to do this is to restructure itself.

Look at the cases below and answer the questions that follow.

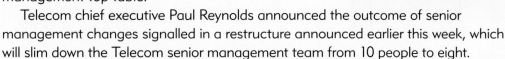

CASE STUDY

Telecom reveals management restructure

Telecom will undertake the next two years' restructuring under its 'Vision 2013' with no human resources department at the company's senior management top table.

Telecom chief executive Paul Reynolds announced the outcome of senior management changes signalled in a restructure announced earlier this week, which will slim down the Telecom senior management team from 10 people to eight.

The changes announced today will create a new role in the company – Chief Product Officer who will oversee new products and pricing in anticipation of the new government's ultra-fast broadband project will create.

Telecom also considering splitting into two companies if it is chosen to act as a government partner to provide ultra-fast broadband to all urban areas by 2018. However, the move today was considered essential to ensure cost reductions and improved commercial performance.

April 2011

Senior Business Studies   ISBN 9780170215732

Kraft slims down as cookie market cracks

Just over a year after taking over Cadbury, Kraft plans to sell off a number of older brands.

The market for snacks has been growing at a greater rate and new markets are showing more positive signs, leading the industry giant to the conclusion that investors will react favourably to a separate business unit.

Kraft's grocery brands – Philadelphia cheese, Jell-O, Maxwell House coffee and its brand of macaroni and cheese – will be grouped together and a new company will be split off from Kraft's snack division.

Their portfolio of brands currently includes Oreo cookies, Cadbury Creme Eggs, Trident gum, Milka chocolate bars and Tang juice drinks.

Irene Rosenfeld, CEO of Kraft, announced the split yesterday and while it initially confounded many analysts it was nevertheless followed by a sharp increase in Kraft's share price.

'We have now reached a stage in our development with global snacks and grocery businesses in North America in which each will benefit from managing themselves,' said Rosenfeld.

August 2011

Thinking

- In each of the case studies, explain the restructuring which has taken place and the possible reasons why.

- Explain in each of the case studies how both internal and external stakeholders could view the restructuring.

- Can you see any disadvantages to the two business featured from carrying out their organisational restructuring?

People in business: Entrepreneurs, leaders and managers

At the end of this unit you will be able to:

- Explain the role and skills of entrepreneurs, leaders and managers.

We saw in Unit 2 that enterprise is required to satisfy needs and wants of consumers, and to create opportunities for other stakeholders, such as employment opportunities to make local communities economically sustainable. Entrepreneurs also need to take risks, and Unit 2 discussed why risk-taking is an essential part of deciding to start up your own small business.

The question remains, however, about what qualities or skills are required in order to become a successful entrepreneur. Is there a type of person or a personality trait that allows certain individuals to become successful entrepreneurs, when others do not?

When looking at this issue, writers tend to focus on successful entrepreneurs as a way to find out the 'magic secret' behind their achievements. The trend among most of our greatest entrepreneurs appears to be that they learned

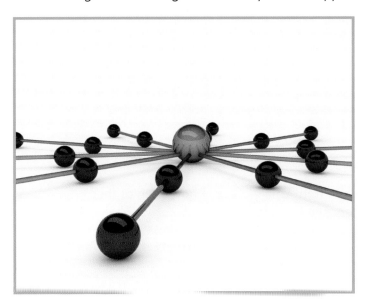

from their mistakes, reviewed their ideas or inventions, and then decided to improve them.

One of New Zealand's most successful entrepreneurs is Owen Glenn. His recommendations give insight into other trends among successful entrepreneurs.

ISBN 9780170215732   Senior Business Studies

Owen Glenn's lessons for success

New Zealand desperately needs people with the skills, ideas and passion to allow us to profitably connect with the world. We need people with entrepreneurial and management skills to grow existing enterprises and new start-ups into global markets.

In our universities and institutes of technology we need to bridge the gap between science, technology and business by ensuring graduates are business informed.

The stories of entrepreneurial scientists such as Colin Green, Paul Callaghan and Garth Smith and entrepreneurs such as Diane Foreman, Jeremy Moon, Derek Handley, Julie Christie, Sir Richard Taylor, Rod Drury and Greg Cross should become compulsory reading.

August 2011

ACTIVITY

Research

- Choose three of the business leaders identified above to find out their business successes and views on being an entrepreneur. Try to research entrepreneurial skills that are needed across different industries

    – What qualities and skills do you think these entrepreneurs have?

    – Do you notice any similarities or differences in their skill set?

Review

- By using the following terms from Unit 2, explain how each of the entrepreneurs you have chosen have demonstrated:

    – Enterprise and innovation.

    – The ability to take and manage risks.

Leadership: the role of leaders and managers

'The foundation of effective leadership is thinking through the organisation's mission, defining it and establishing it, clearly and visibly.'

(Peter Drucker)

Leadership has very strong links to communication, organisational culture and motivation, and is considered to be very different to management.

We can also apply the Māori concept of **rangatiratanga**, defined as chieftainship or leading a group of people. From our previous case study on Dawn Raid (page 55), Brotha D demonstrated rangatiratanga through his willingness to lead the company out of liquidation, admit his mistakes, and still have the determination to carry on.

Leadership models

There are three basic leadership models, which are examined in detail in the table below:

1 Autocratic.

2 Democratic.

3 Laissez-faire.

Style	Description
Autocratic	Sole leader or chief authority figure makes all decisions. There is little or no consultation. The armed forces, government departments or organisations with tall hierarchies may run along autocratic lines.
Democratic	Decisions are made only after consultation has been carried out. This is popular form of leadership style in New Zealand, especially when stakeholders such as a local iwi need to be consulted about a business decision affecting their community.
Laissez-faire	Effectively there is no overall leadership. Individuals may be given a goal or objective and then allowed to decide for themselves the best way forward. Universities tend to be organised under this leadership style.

It should be noted that the autocratic leadership style – usually thought of as largely unfair, uniform/static and unimaginative – can actually bring about higher levels of productivity and wages in some industries. Autocratic leaders are also very practical when a crisis or other emergency occurs.

ISBN 9780170215732

Senior Business Studies

Most of us automatically align ourselves to the democratic style of leadership, however, decision-making by committee or consultation is also the most time consuming and expensive. In certain situations one could argue that a decision may not ever be made.

Laissez-faire leadership, it must be remembered, does not mean being totally free. This style of leading others actually demands a high level of personal responsibility. It normally requires individuals to understand that personal objectives must not take priority over organisational ones.

Personality traits and the importance of charisma

Trait leadership is one of the oldest methods of classifying leadership and has its origins in the work of Plato, who defined the leader as one who possesses a number of key characteristics or particular personality traits that distinguish them from others. These characteristics include but are not limited to:

- Intelligence.
- Reliability.
- Determination.
- Physical presence.
- Ability and being respected for that ability.
- Able to foster new talent or mentoring members of the group.
- Charisma.
- Decisiveness.

It is no longer enough for a corporate boss to be intelligent and good at giving orders. Modern workers may not put up with a hard-nosed, old-fashioned boss like Jack Welch, who used to run General Electric. Typically, workers respond better to leaders who communicate warmly: Indra Nooyi of PepsiCo sometimes writes to the parents of her managers to thank them for bringing up such fine children.

All employees crave a sense of purpose, and the boss who can supply it will get the best out of them. Personal stories also help: Steve Jobs and Sir Richard Branson, whose business empires depend on their charisma, both use strong visions to help motivate employees.

Lady Gaga and Mother Teresa, for instance, both have charisma. This is an important attribute to have in business and in being a leader. Celebrities can tell us something about how charisma can be used. Consider the following case study from *The Economist*.

ISBN 9780170215732

Senior Business Studies

Mother Teresa and Lady Gaga are the latest icons of the leadership industry. Don't laugh

There are obvious differences, of course. Lady Gaga's raw meat dress would probably not have appealed to Mother Teresa of Calcutta. The pop star's habit of changing from one bizarre costume to another several times a day, and maybe 20 times during a gig, might have struck the late nun as extravagant. Mother Teresa wore the same outfit every day: a white sari with three blue stripes, reflecting her vows of poverty, chastity and obedience.

Yet the differences between the two women may matter less than their similarities. Both are widely regarded. Mother Teresa built her Missionaries of Charity from nothing into a global operation with fingers in over 100 countries. Lady Gaga is forecast to earn over $100m in 2011 and may soon outstrip super groups like U2. Both women are also role models for corporate leaders, according to two recent publications, 'Mother Teresa, CEO', a book by two executives, Ruma Bose and Lou Faust, and 'Lady Gaga: Born This Way?' a case study by Jamie Anderson and Jörg Reckhenrich of Antwerp Management School and Martin Kupp of the European School of Management and Technology.

As the two publications argue, both women succeeded by developing simple, clear brands, which coincidentally both identified with outsiders. Mother Teresa ministered to the poor and the sick: people 'shunned by everyone'. Lady Gaga describes herself as 'a freak, a maverick, and a lost soul looking for peers.' She assures her fans that it is OK to be odd. This is a comforting for most teenagers.

Hard work helped both women excel. Mother Teresa rose every day at 4.40am for mass. Lady Gaga 'will take Christmas Day off — and spend it with her parents — but otherwise she works non-stop.' Brilliant communication helped even more. Mother Teresa was a 'Public Relations machine' that, whether talking to a dying leper or a rich donor, 'always left her imprint by communicating in a language the other person understood.' Lady Gaga is 'one of the first pop stars to have truly built her career through the Internet and social media.'

June 2011

Senior Business Studies   ISBN 9780170215732

Situational leadership

Although the trait model has been useful for many years, subsequent management research has found that many of the world's most famous leaders actually lack many of the desirable qualities described previously. New approaches were therefore investigated, leading to work by Frederick Fielder called the 'situational approach'.

The basis of situational leadership is that the situation in which the leader is trying to lead is more important – rather than any character attribute they may possess or the leadership style that is used. The situation in which the leader is trying to lead may be a reflection of the task itself, or the particular make-up of the group.

Fielder attached a great deal of importance to this last point:

> The leader is followed and obeyed not because of rank or power, but due to the positive group emotions such as loyalty, liking, trust and respect.

ACTIVITY

Review

- From the previous case study, identify the leadership qualities of both women.

- Mother Teresa and Lady Gaga could both be said to have mana. How did they achieve this?

- Explain why good communication is so important to good leadership.

- Explain why good leadership relies on the leader having a clear vision.

Research

- Choose a famous sporting event and identify the leader involved on (or off) the field and try to explain how the leader's reactions during the match influenced the final outcome. Did the leader or captain show the right approach to leadership because of their individual qualities, or were they reacting to the situation playing out before them?

Management and managers

'Leaders do things right, managers do the right things.'

(Edward Russell-Walling)

'Skilled managers add to productivity and profitability by creating an environment in which innovation and skill development can flourish.'

(Owen Glenn)

We need to bear in mind the distinction between leadership and management. Other research in this area has helped to identify the ways managers are different to other types of leaders. Gabriel (1998) identifies five key functions of managers:

- Planning a suitable course of action.

- Organising the human and material resources.

- Manpower planning, including recruitment.

- Controlling performance.

- Motivating and encouraging workers to achieve goals.

This last point is important as it represents what most consider to be the most vital attribute that a successful manager should possess. Managers need to be able to recognise the type of worker that they have and then provide the right environment for them to achieve their goals.

McGregor's theory (below) identified two types of workers. Theory X and Theory Y workers have two separate attitudes and abilities towards work. Managers then had to identify the best way to manage and motivate different types of workers. We will be looking at motivation in greater detail in Unit 22.

Theory X Worker:

- Lacks integrity
- Avoids responsibility
- Prefers direction
- Works as little as possible
- Needs supervision
- Motivated by extrinsic methods eg. wages

Theory Y Worker:

- Has integrity
- Works towards responsibility
- Wants to achieve
- Will make decisions and embraces responsibility
- Motivated by intrinsic methods eg. personal growth, job enrichment

ISBN 9780170215732

Senior Business Studies

Communication

21

At the end of this unit you will be able to:

- Identify the purpose of internal and external communication.
- Fully explain what is meant by effective business communication.

Level 2 students without prior Level 1 knowledge are advised to read this section as it provides useful background material that can be applied in the following topic areas:

- Organisational structure and culture.
- Leadership and management.
- Motivation.

The purpose of communication in business

Internal communication

Within any organisation, the need to communicate effectively with internal stakeholders is crucial. The kind of important messages that need to be communicated within either small or large businesses include:

- The objectives, mission and purpose of the organisation.
- Information about promotion opportunities for workers.
- Notices about staff changes or new developments on the business plan affecting all workers.
- What to do and who to contact in the event of an accident or crisis.
- Information about forthcoming events.
- Discussions around a new vision.

ISBN 9780170215732

A summary of internal communication methods is given in the table below. A mix of examples from the business and educational sectors is provided to contextualise each method.

Communication method	Example	Effectiveness
Oral	A manager asking a worker to work overtime at the weekend.	Manager can gain instant reaction and can discuss any issues arising. The process can be two-way. However, this can be time consuming if the manager has to ask 40 workers.
Written Creative Business 45 O'Reilly Road info@creativebusiness.co.nz (09) 456 1300 Please book your Christmas annual leave with Robyn by 10 Nov. Days Available: Rebecca 10 Richard 5 Shane 7 Karen 12 No guarantee that we will be able to meet dates if your application is received after the 10th.	A memo or notice is posted on a notice board either in a business or at school.	Able to be seen by many at one time. A hard copy can be kept on file for reference if there is any confusion, or can be attached to an email and sent at little cost. However, it is only one way with no discussion or feedback possible unless another method is used. Could be viewed as impersonal if a sensitive issue is displayed, for instance, job losses.
Visual	A picture or image is used to convey a warning or give directions.	Can be very cost effective as a way of ensuring health and safety at work. Research shows that warning signs in red are very effective. However, what if some people still do not see it!
Non-verbal	Communicating through facial expressions, gestures or other forms of body language.	Not as effective as it should be given that managers may misread body language. It could be open to different interpretations. There are also significant cultural issues here (see Barriers to communication, page 151).

ISBN 9780170215732

Communication method	Example	Effectiveness
Informal methods, the 'grapevine'	Rumour, gossip, or conversations between staff outside the control of management.	Unreliable and can cause offence and distress, however, management may also use the grapevine to get feedback or ideas from workers on improvements in the production process.
Electronic methods, including social media and texting	The use of mobile technology or social networking sites like Facebook, Twitter and Google +1.	Assumes that people will be able to access the message easily. Reach is considerable at low or no cost. Problems around 'too much' communication being seen by too many. Email over-use or abusive texts are a problem impacting on employee rights. Cost of providing the technological hardware and issues of distraction using social media sites.

Review

- Play a couple of rounds of 'Chinese Whispers' during your lesson. Why does the message at the end of the chain never quite match the message given at the start? What does the activity Chinese Whispers highlight about some of the problems of communicating via the grapevine or through gossip?

Discussion

- Review the main methods that you, as a student, communicate with your friends. Are they always effective? Why or why not?
- How effective is Facebook as a method of communication?

Research

- Review the main methods your school communicates both internally and externally to your school's stakeholders. Explain each of the methods and discuss whether they are effective or not. From this discussion you may be able to generate some useful ideas, which could help improve communication in your school.

External communication

In addition to communicating internally, businesses (and especially schools) have to communicate with their external stakeholders. There are a number of reasons for this.

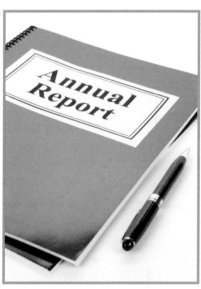

- Publicity about business activities could bring additional customers and lead to greater revenue. This publicity may also ensure that the community views the business positively. Word of mouth promotion can be a positive and effective marketing tool with only a low cost.

- Business success can be reported externally to allow the business to illustrate a point of difference from its competitors. Schools naturally like to publicise the achievements of their students whether academically, on the sports field or in the performing arts.

- Large businesses in New Zealand have to report their financial position to the IRD for tax purposes, and corporation tax has to be paid on all profits earned.

- With Internet, online print and social media now so widespread, businesses have been forced to be more 'transparent' around their business activities. There is an expectation that businesses will now communicate their values and beliefs to show that they are responsible and ethical when dealing with their stakeholders.

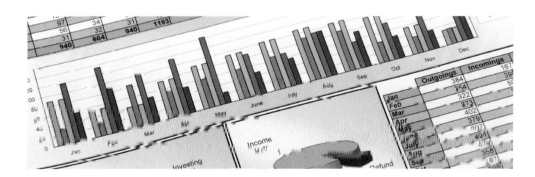

ISBN 9780170215732

Businesses need to be careful around the type of external information they wish to make public. A small business would be unlikely to divulge information about costing and pricing methods or the production processes, since their competitors could use this to their advantage.

Many firms now publish accounts to show how the business is performing. In many countries this is a legal requirement. These accounts are summaries of financial success or failure, and are usually written in such a way to satisfy the requirements of government legislation, yet also to not give away any commercially sensitive information.

CASE STUDY >>>

New store lifts Kathmandu's Newmarket profile

Outdoor retailer Kathmandu is preparing to move into a large, multi-level site in Auckland's Newmarket that has been vacant since teenage outfitter Supre moved out at the start of this year.

Chief executive Peter Halkett said the 1291sq m Broadway site, near the Rialto shopping centre, would become one of the NZX-listed firm's biggest stores in New Zealand.

The company plans to set up shop in time for a pre-Christmas opening.

Christchurch-based Kathmandu reported a 24.5 per cent lift in sales to $306 million this week, while pre-tax earnings for the period were expected to be up by as much as 36 per cent.

Halkett said Kathmandu had spent years looking for a 'more prime' Newmarket site than its present one upstairs near Broadway's intersection with Remuera Rd.

The original Newmarket site will be kept open as an outlet store.

August 2011

ACTIVITY

Discussion

- Identify the key information from the case study that the Kathmandu CEO has decided to communicate to its stakeholders.

- Do you think that there is any 'commercially sensitive' information contained in this article? If not, why not?

Senior Business Studies   ISBN 9780170215732

- Explain why Kathmandu decided to announce the opening of their new store in August even though it is not expected to open until Christmas 2011.

Research

- Interview a senior manager of your school to find out the benefits and costs to your school from having a website. How effective is the external communication? (One possible Level 2 activity for a group could be to plan and suggest improvements in the school's external communication, carry the plans out and then gather feedback in order to refine it and improve it further.)

Barriers to effective communication

Effective communication can be defined as when **both the receiver of a message and its sender agree** on the contents and/or on any future action that needs to occur to either resolve issues or clarify what needs to happen next. Communication that is ineffective, therefore, is either misunderstood, unacknowledged or not acted on.

Despite all the various internal and external methods used by business to communicate, there are several barriers to effective communication.

- **The use of technical jargon**
  The sender of the message should not assume that the receiver understands all the technical information included in a letter or email.

- **The length of the message or imprecise language used**
  If a communication method takes too long to deliver a message it may confuse the receiver or the message may be ignored. The email delete button is easy to locate. A long memo may be irritating to the receiver and they may simply put it in the recycle bin.

- **Misunderstanding the emotional impact of the communication**
  The email you sent as a joke might be taken badly by the receiver, or ignored. Or a manager may decide to send a letter to a subordinate over a discipline issue rather than speak to them face to face. Because the communication method is one-way, the worker may become angry that they have not had the opportunity to defend themselves.

ISBN 9780170215732

Cultural communication barriers

As New Zealand businesses strive to develop their presence in the global marketplace, communicating across different countries and time zones occurs more frequently. We need to be aware of any cultural etiquette that is appropriate, as these can have significant impact on the way information needs to be transmitted and interpreted.

- The importance of 'saving face' in Japanese culture cannot be overlooked. A worker may say, 'Yes I understand' to a question rather than 'No, I don't' (even if their true answer is no), as the worker wishes to retain their dignity and avoid the embarrassment of not knowing the answer.

- Singaporeans have an expression called 'kiasu' or 'scared to lose', which is similar to saving face when confronted with an issue they do not quite understand. In situations such as these, body language is a good indicator of their answer to a question.

- Tactile displays of emotion such as hugging and kissing on both cheeks is regarded as an important part of any business conversation in Saudi Arabia or the Gulf states.

- Falling asleep in business meetings would be considered rude in New Zealand, however it is not uncommon in Japan. Silences and reflecting on a question – pauses in communication – are also an important part of business etiquette.

ACTIVITY

Research

- Take the perspective of each of the four main cultural identities in New Zealand – New Zealand European, Māori, Asian, and Pacific – to look into other forms of cultural etiquette that can impact on effective communication.

Discussion

- Do you think that the use of technology has made communication more or less effective in New Zealand?

ISBN 9780170215732

Senior Business Studies

Motivation

At the end of this unit you will be able to:

- Explain and discuss key motivation theories.

The purpose of motivation

Motivation can be thought of as the desire and willingness to achieve your goals. Fredrick Herzberg neatly summarised motivation as the process of *wanting* to do a good job rather than *having* to.

In this way, Herzberg makes the crucial distinction of motivation being **intrinsic**. The desire to do a good job comes from within the person, rather than them being forced to do so by **extrinsic** methods like increasing pay or threats by management. Extrinsic management has sometimes been referred to as the 'carrot and the big stick' approach.

How to motivate their subordinates is the dilemma for all managers in business.

- Do we encourage or threaten?

- Do increasing salaries and wages motivate, or are there other factors at work that compel workers to 'do a good job'?

- How important is non-financial motivation such as teamwork, time off work or job satisfaction?

Senior Business Studies   ISBN 9780170215732

Rugby: Graham Henry irked by young talent heading offshore

All Black coach Graham Henry is annoyed that young players surrender their international rugby chances for large offshore contracts.

That exasperation shone through yesterday as Henry applauded Keven Mealamu's decision to sign on for another two years of rugby in New Zealand.

Mealamu is 32 and joins a growing list of senior players who have signed on past the World Cup, content to develop his business, family and personal interests in New Zealand instead of chasing contracts in Europe.

The 83-test All Black felt uneasy about moving overseas. 'This is a special place and I thought it would be hard to play for any other team,' he said yesterday.

As the conversation shifted, Henry revealed how disturbed he was at the exit of players on the verge of international selection.

'It irritates me the guys outside the All Black squad who have a dream about being an All Black for 25 years and then all of a sudden they get offered $500,000 from overseas and bugger off and don't fulfill the dream.'

He could not understand why players would leave New Zealand when they were so close to their sporting goals.

'That does irritate me, the young guys who have had a dream for 15 to 20 years, give up the dream because they get offered some big money to go to Ireland or France or somewhere, and they finish up regretting it.'

Henry did not believe a significant number of All Blacks would leave after this year's World Cup but he was concerned about the impending departures of those close to making the All Black squads.

April 2011

ISBN 9780170215732

ACTIVITY

Review

- What is Graham Henry referring to as 'the dream'?

- Write down two reasons why a New Zealand rugby player would want to follow this dream.

- Given your answer above, why are so many potential All Black players deciding to play the game overseas?

- Describe two solutions to the problems of retaining future All Black players to play in New Zealand.

- Using the case study, explain the most important motivation factor for potential All Blacks.

Discussion

- What is your motivation for studying this business course?

Motivation theories

This unit will apply several theories of motivation to find some answers. Only brief outlines of the background research will be supplied, as it is expected that students will research these theories themselves in greater detail:

- Maslow's Hierarchy or Pyramid of Needs.

- Taylor's scientific approach, The Economic Man.

- Mayo's Hawthorne Effect.

- Herzberg's Two-factor Theory.

- Vroom and Adams Expectancy Theory.

Abraham Maslow: Hierarchy of Needs

Many students will be familiar with the pyramid of needs defined by Abraham Maslow in his research of motivation conducted in the 1950s. Using this pyramid (see following page), one could argue that from the previous case study that becoming an All Black or Tall Fern or All White implies that you have reached your self-actualisation. You have made it!

Note in the diagram that Maslow's pyramid has been updated for the new century. 'Transcendence' is the modern focus of motivation – helping others achieve their 'All Black' moment.

Maslow's ideas around motivation centre mostly on satisfying needs. At the bottom of the pyramid, basic needs and wants have to be satisfied before an individual is motivated to move to the next level of safety.

When individuals feel safe they are then motivated to try and achieve Love and Belonging, and the process continues.

ISBN 9780170215732

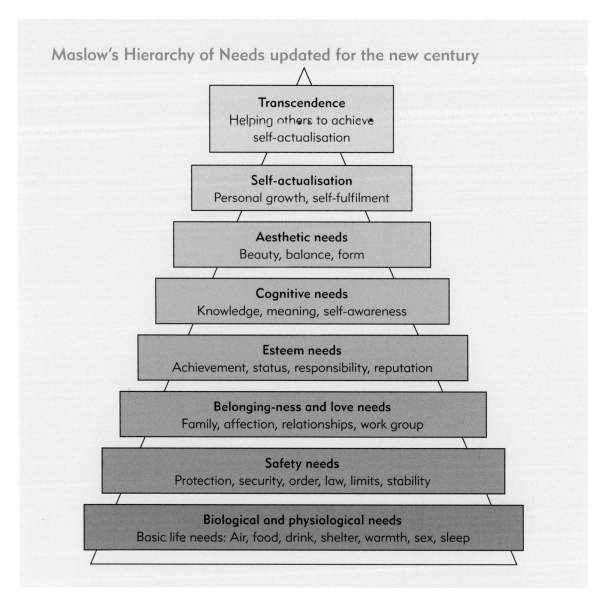

Maslow's Hierarchy of Needs updated for the new century

Transcendence
Helping others to achieve self-actualisation

Self-actualisation
Personal growth, self-fulfilment

Aesthetic needs
Beauty, balance, form

Cognitive needs
Knowledge, meaning, self-awareness

Esteem needs
Achievement, status, responsibility, reputation

Belonging-ness and love needs
Family, affection, relationships, work group

Safety needs
Protection, security, order, law, limits, stability

Biological and physiological needs
Basic life needs: Air, food, drink, shelter, warmth, sex, sleep

F.W. Taylor: The Economic Man

Before Maslow's work, F.W. Taylor created the first substantial theory around motivation at the beginning of the twentieth century. He argued that individual jobs should be thoroughly analysed and reviewed, and that standards of performance be measured.

Workers who regularly achieved the standard would be paid a fixed wage, and those who over performed would receive a bonus. Workers who consistently underperformed would eventually be replaced. At its most basic level, Taylor's ideas assumed that workers were motivated by the 'carrot and big stick' idea.

Senior Business Studies   ISBN 9780170215732

Elton Mayo: The Hawthorne Effect

Many entrepreneurs took up Taylor's scientific approach to management enthusiastically during the industrial age of the early twentieth century. One in particular was Henry Ford, who enjoyed enormous economic success in applying these ideas to flow production (see Unit 17) of motorcars, his most famous product being the Model T Ford.

However, some came to doubt the power of money as a motivator. In the 1930s Elton Mayo conducted a number of experiments around motivation in teams and found some startling results. A full discussion is not given here and students are encouraged to research Mayo's work for themselves.

In essence, he discovered that workers are committed to completing a task as a group, and especially if they have had some input into the decision-making process. Money was not their key motivator. These results led the investigation of other human (non-financial) methods of motivation.

Frederick Herzberg: The Two-factor Theory

Herzberg's theory is represented diagrammatically below.

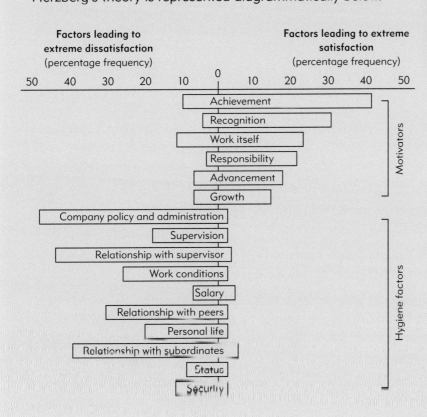

Semo · Business Studies   ISBN 9780170215732

Victor Vroom: Expectancy Theory

Vroom's work theorised that an employee's performance is based on a range of individual factors such as experience, personality, skills and abilities.

Expectancy theory says that individuals have different sets of goals and are motivated when there is a positive correlation between their effort and favourable performance leading to a desired reward, receiving a reward that satisfies an important need, or when the desire to satisfy the need is strong enough to make the effort worthwhile.

Review

- Draw a Maslow Pyramid for a teacher or a nurse. Identify each specific need. Fully explain whether you think the Maslow Pyramid fits the motivation of a teacher or nurse. Compare your answer with a fellow student or teacher. Are there any similarities or differences?

- Draw a Maslow Pyramid for Lady Gaga or Mother Teresa and comment on your results.

- How does Taylor's theory apply to NCEA Achievement Standards such as Not Achieved, Achieved, Merit and Excellence?

- Despite significant differences in resources and experiences, the US beat England in World Cup Soccer for the first time ever in 1950. Explain how the Hawthorne Effect could have been a motivating factor in this or any other sporting upset.

- Some great teachers never wish to become principals or part of the senior management team. Use a Maslow Pyramid to explain why some workers may not wish to reach the 'top'.

Senior Business Studies   ISBN 9780170215732

ISBN 9780170215732

ACTIVITY

Research

Watch the following YouTube clip called 'Jumping for the Jelly Beans Parts 1 and 2', that usefully explains Herzberg's theory on motivation.

- Why does Herzberg argue that the worst way to motivate someone to play the piano is to pay them?

- What does Herzberg suggest are the best two ways to motivate someone to play the piano?

Discussion

- Many people enter *American Idol* or television reality contests such as the *X Factor* or *Britain's Got Talent* in the expectation that they are going to win. Many have very high Vroom expectancy. When the inevitable disappointment arrives and they are eliminated from the competition, the reaction is usually tearful, anger or denial. Given Vroom's Expectancy Theory, why do so many continue to enter these competitions despite the inevitable disappointment? Is Vroom's theory wrong in this situation?

Putting these theories into context: a brief discussion

- Maslow's Pyramid has been challenged, as the original model assumed that all workers wish to move up through the levels of need. Some, like artists (and teachers!), however, may choose to sacrifice lower order Maslow needs such as physiological or security – by refusing to take a higher paying steady job, for example – in order to pursue another endeavour.

- Taylor's Scientific theory has been described as autocratic and old fashioned. However, as we saw in the units on leadership and organisational structure, there may be very good reason why management may choose to measure performance and/or restructure a large business, especially if the external environment is changing. (As we will outline in Unit 23, an 'Apollonian' culture within large business may lead to increased productivity in times of a crisis.)

- Herzberg's Hygiene factors are not motivators but it would be wrong of managers to neglect them. If working conditions are not satisfactory to the work force then motivators such as achievement, responsibility and personal growth are not possible.

Sen● Business Studies

Non-financial motivation

Herzberg's studies revealed the limitations of money or financial motivation. Daniel Pink's excellent YouTube clip 'The Surprising Truth about what motivates us' on this issue reflects on why non-financial motivation may be more powerful. He argues that the creation and sustainability of Wikipedia is a classic example of why individuals choose to be motivated by other things than just money.

As a result, and in combination with work from McGregor (Theory X and Y), **job enrichment** theories around motivation were developed. His research supported the idea that if workers obtain new skills they can 'grow' in their job, and become more productive. As Herzberg himself put it, 'the more someone can do, the more you can motivate them.'

Respect, **promotion** and **opportunity** are now considered to be key motivators in the job enrichment approach. In particular, McGregor's study argues that Theory Y managers are motivated by responsibility and the ability to make one's own decisions. Theory X managers need to supervise and monitor, whereas Theory Y need freedom and recognition.

In the new economy, businesses are now having to examine traditional motivational practices and come up with new ways to retain their workers. There is an excellent YouTube clip by Gary Hamel (Reinventing Management for the 21st Century) looking at new ways to manage and motivate in the new economy, and contains many excellent ideas on non-financial motivation.

The ideas of Herzberg and McGregor have had significant impacts on the type of organisational culture of new businesses. It is to this topic that we now turn.

ISBN 9780170215732

ACTIVITY

Research (Level 2)

- As part of Internal Assessment AS 90844 you will be required to carry out a review and evaluation of motivational practices in a workplace of a large company of regional or national significance. (See www.tki.org.nz for more details.)

Organisational culture

At the end of this unit you will be able to:

- Explain organisational culture and its impact on leadership and motivation.
- Explain why culture clashes may occur with an organisation.

This unit links information from the units on leadership, communication and motivation. We will also be referring to the work of Charles Handy. In his book *Gods of Management*, Handy tries to classify the different types of culture that can exist within a business.

Definition

An **organisational culture** is the attitudes, beliefs, experiences and values that underpin the working relationships between internal and external stakeholders.

No one business has just one culture, and the reality is that organisations are made up of individuals from different backgrounds with different needs and aspirations. Sometimes these cultures may clash. It is the job of senior management to ensure that these clashes are managed in the most effective way.

The organisational culture should be thought of as a reflection of the organisation's mission and vision, and the type of leadership and management structures in place. There is no such thing as a 'correct' organisational culture. For some businesses an open, relaxed or informal culture is appropriate, but for others a more disciplined and structured culture is better suited.

Before we classify organisational culture further let us get a greater sense of what organisational culture is by having a closer look at a particular company's culture.

Senior Business Studies   ISBN 9780170215732

The Google culture

Though Google has grown a lot since it first began in 1998, we still maintain a small company feel.

At lunchtime, almost everyone eats in the office café, sitting at whatever table has an opening and enjoying conversations with Googlers from different teams. Our commitment to innovation depends on everyone being comfortable sharing ideas and opinions. Every employee is a hands-on contributor, and everyone wears several hats. Because we believe that each Googler is an equally important part of our success, no one hesitates to pose questions directly to Larry or Sergey in our weekly all-hands ('TGIF') meetings – or spike volleyball across the net at a corporate officer.

We are aggressively inclusive in our hiring, and we favor ability over experience. We have offices around the world and Google staffers speak dozens of languages, from Turkish to Telugu. The result is a team that reflects the global audience Google serves. When not at work, Googlers pursue interests from cross-country cycling to wine tasting, from flying to frisbee.

As we continue to grow, we are always looking for those who share a commitment to creating search perfection and having a great time doing it.

About our offices: Here are a few things you might see in a Google workspace.

- Bicycles or scooters for efficient travel between meetings; dogs; lava lamps; massage chairs; large inflatable balls.
- Googlers sharing cubes, yurts and huddle rooms – and very few solo offices.
- Laptops everywhere – standard issue for mobile coding, email on the go and note-taking.
- Foosball, pool tables, volleyball courts, assorted video games, pianos, ping-pong tables, and gyms that offer yoga and dance classes.
- Grassroots employee groups for all interests like meditation, film, wine tasting and salsa dancing.
- Healthy lunches and dinners for all staff at a variety of cafés.
- Break rooms packed with a variety of snacks and drinks to keep Googlers going.

ISBN 9780170215732

ACTIVITY

Review

- Describe the Google culture, in your own words.

- Google is one of the most innovative companies in the world. From your study of Unit 2 explain how the Google culture may lead to workers (or 'Googlers') being innovative.

- Who are Larry and Sergey?

- Would you call the principal of your school by their first name? Explain your answer.

- Do you think that the Google culture may be appropriate in your own school or college?

- How much profit did Google make last year?

- How much is the company worth in terms of sale and, assets owned (or market capitalisation)?

Classifiying organisational a culture

There are many different ways to classify cultures. One of the most popular is from Charles Handy's book *The Gods of Management*, which uses four ancient Greek gods to define four (there may be more!) different types of culture. The connections between culture and motivation are explained in more detail in the table that follows.

- **Zeus** cultures may refer to a family business, with the elders of the family or whanau having started it. Ownership, control and continuity is determined by the family.

- **Apollo** cultures are typical of highly structured companies run along autocratic or bureaucratic lines. Examples include the armed forces and other organisations with strict policies and procedures in place.

- **Athenean** cultures are creative and problem solving cultures, very popular in the media and technology industries such as film, television and advertising.

- Individual (existential) cultures represented by **Dionysus** exist when there is no overall leadership. Due to their experience or reputation workers are left to work independently, but they are expected to produce work or contribute to the overall mission of the organisation. Personal responsibility is very important. It is not a 'free' or 'do what you want' culture.

Senior Business Studies

	Zeus	Apollo	Athena	Dionysus
Symbol				
Culture	Club. Similar to strong.	Role. Similar to strong.	Task or problem solving. Open but strong as deadline approaches.	Individualistic. Relaxed and open.
Example of business	Family business such as New Zealand farm or winery.	Local government.	Media and software companies.	Universities.
Example of worker in this culture	Farm owner or any entrepreneur.	Accountant, tax auditor, immigration officer.	Advertising executive. Film maker.	ICT specialist, some teachers and nurses.
Leadership style appropriate to culture	Paternalistic (father figure). At the head of the family.	Autocratic and bureaucratic.	Democratic.	Do not wish to be managed. Flexible/laissez faire.
Individual characteristics	Charismatic, impulsive, hardworking, optimistic.	Thoughtful, reliable, rational.	Sociable, anxious to solve problems, extrovert.	Rigid, introverted, reserved but loyal.
Ways to motivate	Feeds on power and influence. Financial success allows more risk taking. Values networks and connections.	Promotion based on work ethic. Recognition for work done. 'Moving up the corporate hierarchy'.	Opportunities to work in Matrix structures and solve new problems. Training to learn new skills.	Allowed to get on with their job due to respect afforded by their other colleagues.
Issues	Easily irritated by rules and regulations. Likes to be proactive than reactive in business.	Inflexibility? Hates too much change. Perceived as difficult but can be excellent in a crisis situation.	Can be indecisive in a crisis. Irritated by certainty. Needs constant challenges or gets bored.	Can be viewed as selfish. The organisation is regarded as a way to help the individual and not the other way round.

Culture clash

Note the number of potential sources of conflict and culture clashes in the table opposite. These are natural in large businesses as all workers and managers are different. The key to cultural balance is how these differences can be managed.

- **Zeus's** may become irritated with Apollos insistence on sticking to the rules. Zeus's may be viewed as power hungry and always looking at vision rather than the day-to-day detail of business.

- **Apollos** may be accused of lacking flair and imagination, or having too much of a focus on getting the job done. Zeus' may grudgingly admit that they need Apollos to save them from bureaucracy.

- **Athenians** may become bored and leave an organisation if they are not feeling challenged. An Athenian in an Apollo culture may lead to poor productivity.

- **Dionysians** may be loyal and highly productive, but they are notoriously difficult to manage.

ACTIVITY

Research

- Carry out some individual investigations into Summerhill, a private school in the UK. How would you describe the culture there? What are the problems for a New Zealand school trying to introduce a culture similar to Summerhill? You may also wish to research Orimiston Senior College and Albany Senior College as examples from New Zealand of different school cultures.

- One of the most famous culture clashes in recent business history is the failed merger between two very powerful media companies, America Online and Time Warner. Find out what happened when decided to merge, and what happened that led to one of the biggest corporate losses ever.

- Undertake some research into Pixar. It has been called 'the dream factory'. It is an enterprise that produces award-winning animated and computer generated films. Pixar has a very open culture but it is also driven by commercial success. Look at the reasons why Pixar has been so successful.

Discussion

- Comment on Google's financial performance for 2011. How can the business, which gives away over 90% of its services for free, be so profitable and so wealthy?

ISBN 9780170215732

24 Recruitment

At the end of this unit you will be able to:

- Identify effective processes for the recruitment of employees.

Definition

Recruitment is a process that turns the need for a new employee into a successful appointment. The Māori concept of **tikanga** applies to the ethics of recruiting.

Most leaders and managers would agree that one of their most important roles is to find the right person to fit the job. It could be a new role required by the business, or to replace an existing worker who has moved on.

Recruitment is a very important issue in small businesses, as an inappropriate appointment has the potential to disrupt teamwork.

Unlike large businesses, small firms may not have a separate human resource department. This means that the recruitment function must be carried out by the owner of the business. Faced with the opportunity costs of advertising, finding, interviewing and then selecting a new person, many small business owners rely on friends and family to find new or replacement workers.

ISBN 9780170215732

The recruitment process

A typical process of recruitment includes the following steps:

- Identifying the need for a new job by carrying out a **job analysis**.

- Drawing up a **job description** and a **person specification**.

- Advertising the vacancy in the local media or online websites such as www.seek.co.nz.

- Gathering application forms, **curriculum vitae** and references to allow the business to **shortlist** potential candidates.

- Selecting the candidate by conducting interviews, and in some cases asking candidates to perform some tasks such as psychometric or aptitude tests.

- **Welcoming**, **inducting** and **training** the successful candidate into the ways of the business.

Cultural considerations

In Asian and Māori cultures, recruiting exclusively within the family or whanau is an important protocol.

Successful small businesses in particular demand that individuals are able to work well together, so given the close working relationships required, family members may better appreciate, understand and enjoy this environment rather than new recruits from outside the family.

Family businesses frequently recruit future managers and leaders from within the extended family. This has the advantage of reducing the costs of recruitment, however, it can also unnecessarily exclude fresh ideas from outside the family unit.

The following practice case study for Internal Assessment 90841 (Investigate human resource processes) is fictitious. It has been written to allow students to apply their business knowledge of human resource processes to collect relevant and detailed information that could be useful in helping an entrepreneur solve a human resource problem.

Students are encouraged to research their own answers to the terms mentioned, and discuss some of the issues surrounding successful recruitment, in addition to the questions that follow. The following case study is also applied to business concepts in the next unit.

Senior Business Studies   ISBN 9780170215732

Number 6

Part 1: Background

Number 6 is a restaurant owned by Joe Maxwell. It serves high quality expensive food on the West Coast of the South Island with diners travelling long distances to eat there. Joe, who had set up the restaurant after leaving school with his whanau, had originally started the restaurant as a take-away shop serving quick food. Joe was the head of the company and he had three brothers – Tama, Taylor and Joshua who each had separate roles. Tama looked after the finance as the accountant; Taylor was the main chef and Joshua his shop assistant.

However, in 2003, Joe had taken the brave decision to relaunch his take-away shop as an exclusive restaurant and financed this decision by borrowing heavily from friends and his family. Taylor and Joshua trained for 2 years to acquire new cooking skills. The new restaurant was renamed Number 6 and quickly became a great success and soon had won a number of awards for the quality and presentation of its food. Local celebrities had also begun to visit and in 2007, the restaurant was featured in a TV documentary highlighting Māori business success stories.

By 2011, Joe decided that he needed to look into ways of developing Number 6. He had noticed on a recent trip to Christchurch that there were a large number of Japanese restaurants serving both sushi and cooked meals and they were very busy. He had also researched that Japanese food served in this way was very healthy. Joe had always maintained that the food served at Number 6 should not only be of the finest quality but also be socially responsible. He decided to look into the idea of serving high quality Japanese dishes in his restaurant.

Part 2: The human resource problem

Joe had traditionally employed whanau and friends in his restaurant on a part-time basis when the restaurant was busy but he was unable to find any member of his iwi who had experience of preparing Japanese food. Taylor lacked experience of Japanese cooking and wanted to focus on his existing role. Joe had conducted a **job analysis** of all of the workers and roles at Number 6 but had decided that he needed to recruit externally away from the whanau.

Before he could launch his Japanese menu he needed to find an experienced Japanese cook who could prepare dishes to the standard the customers of Number 6 demanded.

Joe researched a number of websites and local newspapers but was having little luck. He could not find somebody locally and so he decided to place a job advertisement on www.seek.co.nz. He emailed a recruitment agency in Japan offering their services for a small fee. Joe drew up a **job description** and **person specification** and waited for a response.

Part 3: Shortlisting

After two weeks, Joe had received 50 replies. He was very busy at Number 6 and **shortlisted** three candidates who seemed to fit the conclusions of the job analysis.

- Penny: A 25-year-old trainee chef who had experience of working in one of the top restaurants in Auckland. She had been the top graduate from her training programme. She seemed very keen and asked if she could visit Number 6 before she made a full application.

- David: A 55-year-old chef from Nelson who had 20 years experience of working in Asian Food kitchens including a six month part-time job in Japan. He wrote in his application that he wanted to move to the West Coast to be closer to his grandchildren.

- Shinya: A 35-year-old chef who was from Japan but who wanted to come and live in New Zealand. His English language skills were not developed but he had extensive knowledge of Japanese cooking.

Part 4: Selection

Joe telephoned David and spoke for an hour. Penny arrived at Number 6 unannounced and spoke about her passion for Japanese cooking. Shinya had set up a webcam and without asking during their Skype conversation had demonstrated his abilities to Joe using the Internet. All three candidates had significant strengths and Jo was unsure who to finally offer the job to.

Senior Business Studies   ISBN 9780170215732

Part 5: Other factors influencing the decision

Joe felt that he needed more information about this new job at Number 6 before he could offer it. He decided to find out salaries of top Japanese chefs already in Auckland. He also felt that he needed to contact the New Zealand Immigration Department to check to see if he could get a work visa for Shinya if he was appointed. Some members of the whanau who had supported Joe in the beginning of Number 6 were very supportive of his decision to offer high quality Japanese food but were critical of his decision to look outside the whanau to find a top chef.

Joe was concerned that the decision to recruit externally could lead to other human resource issues if his appointment was not accepted by his whanau.

Part 6: Induction training, rights and responsibilities, offer and acceptance

Two further issues remained. Whoever he appointed, Joe knew that he would have to provide some induction training to the successful candidate. Locally this would be difficult to do, so Joe had to include the cost of a training programme in Christchurch and allow for a few weeks for the successful candidate to practice their skills before the new opening.

Secondly, given that all of the current workers in Number 6 had been recruited locally without any previous job descriptions, Joe felt that he needed to draw up an **employment agreement** outlining the **rights** and **responsibilities** of the new employee. Joe had risked a good deal of his capital in Number 6 and the new Japanese menu and wanted to make sure that the business structure was more formal. Neither Tama, Taylor nor Joshua had an employment contract.

Finally, how should he offer the job? The new employment agreement would need to specify the terms and conditions of employment and include reference to the **90-day Bill legislation**, which affected all new employees. Joe felt that needed to get details written down on paper to avoid any future disagreements and in contrast to his previous appointments, he decided to offer and accept the job by letter.

Time was not on Joe's side. He had advertised excitedly on the Number 6 website a new creative and innovative Japanese menu was coming soon. Local interest was growing and the high tourist summer season was approaching where Number 6 made over 70% of their sales revenue.

He needed to appoint the most appropriate person and quickly.

Review

- Define the terms in bold throughout the case study.

- Explain why Joe needed to consult with his whanau before making a final decision. Did Joe follow the correct recruitment process according to tikanga?

- Why do you think that Joe prepared a job description and person specification?

- Explain the importance of outlining the rights and responsibilities of the new employee in an agreement

- Identify one benefit and one cost of recruiting workers using online methods (such as www.seek.co.nz).

- Why would Joe need to conduct thorough induction training?

- Who do you think Joe will appoint and why?

Rights and responsibilities of employers and employees

At the end of this unit you will be able to:

- Outline the rights and responsibilities of the employer and the employee.

Definition

An **employment right** is considered an entitlement when taking a job. The Department of Labour's website (www.dol.govt.nz) has a great deal of information concerning the individual rights of workers in New Zealand. It is the responsibility of the employee to fulfil the obligations of their employment right.

Clearly then, an employee right backed by government legislation becomes an employer **responsibility** or something businesses are obliged to provide.

We saw in the previous unit that a small business such as Number 6 will need to spend a considerable amount of time and energy in finding the best employee for a new position.

However, it is not just a case of finding a suitable candidate. The successful person will need to 'fit' with the existing employees in order to ensure that business operations are not disrupted and that productivity of the business continues. An inappropriate fit not only costs the business money and time, but the whole process of recruitment will have to be repeated, delaying the solution to the human resource issue identified by the job analysis.

Implications of the Number 6 case for rights and responsibilities

The Number 6 case study also revealed that, during the recruitment process, discussions between the new employee and employer would have to contain information about the role being offered, conditions of work, rates of pay and leave or holiday entitlements. These are considered to be the employee's rights.

In addition, the employer would set out his requirements of the new worker, expectations of behaviour, conduct and the routines of the business. This point is crucial since, as of April 2011, the introduction of the 90-Day bill means that a new employee is required to know exactly what is expected of them if they wish to keep their new job beyond the trial period.

A written employment agreement is obviously very important. In the case of disputes, the employee and employer can go back to the original document and then discuss what was agreed at the time of appointment.

Other real life rights and responsibilities highlighted in the case study of Number 6 include:

- A written agreement outlining pay, hours of work and conditions of service.

- Annual holiday entitlements.

- Leave for sickness and for sickness of dependents.

- Health and safety issues within the workplace which need to be noted by both employee and employer and customers if applicable.

- Entitlements to breaks within the working day.

- Rates of overtime pay (if applicable) which are agreed between the parties if the employee works longer than the specified number of hours in the contract.

- Training opportunities both on and off the job.

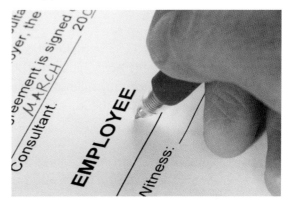

Employee responsibilities

The employee must make a commitment to the workplace they have been recruited to be part of.

- Employees should arrive on time for work.

- Employees cannot simply take a day off because they feel like it. A medical certificate will need to be produced if sick and absent for more than three days.

- Employees should observe the health and safety rules present in the business and be expected to be evaluated on their performance within the company in accordance with the employment contract. This particular process is called appraisal and it could be part of an employer's decision to conduct a job analysis.

- Employees need to be aware of their responsibilities and continue to meet high standards of work expected of them by their employer. Failure to do so may result in the employer have to take some kind of sanction against the employee, or in extreme cases of poor behaviour a worker may be dismissed.

ISBN 9780170215732

Many small businesses now try to keep the relationship between employer and employee as 'informal and constructive' as possible. If a business has less than twenty employees any tension or misunderstanding could have significant impacts on the smooth running of the business. The employer will not wish to waste time and resources looking for a new employee only to have to go through the process again.

On occasion, employees and employers may need to negotiate.

CASE STUDY

Wage loss for snowbound workers

Workers at KFC, Pizza Hut and Starbucks stores in areas badly hit by the polar blast have been told that they will not get paid for any hours lost during the latest snowstorm, a union claims.

The fast-food firms' owner, Restaurant Brands New Zealand, is among companies accused of taking a hard line on workers who have trouble making it to work because of bad weather.

Christchurch Unite Union organiser Matt Jones criticised Restaurant Brands and believed the company was legally obligated to pay staff that had made efforts to get to work but had decided that the trip would be too difficult.

'We understand that the only option left to the staff is to use what annual leave they may have, which is unethical,' Mr Jones said.

A Restaurant Brands spokesman said: 'Staff who turn up to work are paid for the shift. If a staff member turns up to a store but the manager decides to not open, then they will be paid for their normal shift … If the store closes early due to weather safety conditions, the remaining hours of the shift shall be honored … If a staff member decides to not turn up to work as a result of the weather, they will not be paid, but can choose to take leave if they wish … Staff who are genuinely prevented from turning up to work due to the weather conditions will be paid, but confirmation of this is on a case-by-case basis as there need to be genuine reasons.'

Council of Trade Unions secretary Peter Conway said that bad weather was tough on everybody, especially when it interfered with normal operations, but hoped workers would remain on pay even if they could not get to work.

'When the police, transport and Civil Defence agencies are advising people not to travel, it is simply not feasible for workers to make it to work. And to then have pay docked is unfair.'

ISBN 9780170215732

Otago Chamber of Commerce chief executive John Christie said businesses usually included conditions in employment contracts and were entitled to dock pay if staff did not turn up for work.

Mr Christie said it was a difficult situation, which depended on workplace contracts or policies. 'Restaurant Brands are entitled to take the stand they have, but a lot of organisations take a more moderate stance.'

'Some employers have updated their employment contracts given heavy snowfalls from last year and have communicated them to staff. That is good business practice.'

August 2011

Recruitment mistakes and the 90-day Bill

Even though the recruitment process may have been rigorous, and even after all the induction and training has been given, employers may still find that the new employee they hired is not settling into the business as effectively as was hoped. Perhaps the employee's skills have not lived up to the information provided in their application.

Faced with this issue, employers in New Zealand have lobbied the government to step in and help. The resulting legislation was controversial.

National pushes through 90-day work law

Employment law changes, which were fiercely fought by unions and the Labour Party, have been passed by Parliament.

The 90-day trial period for new employees has been extended to all businesses.

Labour Minister Kate Wilkinson said the 90-day trial period, which previously applied to businesses with 20 or fewer employees, had been a success.

It was introduced soon after the 2008 election, with unions very unhappy.

'Rather than being unfair and restricting recruitment, as was hysterically proclaimed, employers of small and medium-sized businesses gained the confidence to hire new employees,' Ms Wilkinson said.

ISBN 9780170215732

Senior Business Studies

'Without the trial period, hundreds of New Zealand workers would not have the jobs they currently do have.'

Ms Wilkinson said employers wanted to invest and grow their businesses but didn't want to face a personal grievance if they hired someone who turned out to be unsuitable. 'They simply chose not to hire anyone. The 90-day trial has changed that.'

Labour MP Trevor Mallard, the party's labour relations spokesman, said extending the trial period was 'just a continuation of the National Party's attack on the rights of wage and salary earners and their conditions ... It would not help the economy and was being done for political and ideological reasons,' he said.

'It weakens the processes around job security, extends the range of reasons for dismissal, restricts substantially the right to appeal, and restricts the right to reinstatement,' Mr Mallard said.

November 2010

ACTIVITY

Review

- Who do you think is correct in the disagreement between employees and their employer in the Restaurant Brands study?

- Explain the importance of having a written agreement.

- Explain why the existence of external factors can make enforcing a written agreement difficult.

- Suggest a solution to the issue raised in the Restaurant Brands study.

Research

- Find out exactly what the 90-day Bill means for new employees and employers.

- The second case study was written in 2010. Try to find out from using online sources whether or not the views expressed have turned out to be true or false.

Thinking

- Explain why the 90-day Bill may lead to 'giving employers the confidence to hire new workers'.

- Explain why Mr Mallard argues that the Bill may lead to a 'weakening' of employee rights.

ISBN 9780170215732

Senior Business Studies

Trade unions and employer associations

At the end of this unit you will be able to:

- Explain the role of trade unions and employer associations and why they may use collective bargaining.

In the previous unit we saw that the 90-day Bill legislation has the potential to generate tension between employers and employees. The bill states that an employer can dismiss a new employee within 90 days without reason.

One could argue that under the new bill an employee now has the opportunity to impress his or her new boss, and that the legislation is simply an attempt to solve some of the awkward situations that can occur when an inappropriate appointment has been made.

Alternatively, there is the argument that many employees will now feel more insecure in the workplace, and given Maslow's hierarchy of needs (see page 156) may become prone to demotivation.

In small businesses (of less than twenty employees), negotiations between the employee and employer should consist of a number of conversations over the course of a year. In this way, conflicts can be addressed quickly.

In larger businesses, however, with hundreds of employees, this process is restricted due to time. Unions were therefore created to help individual workers negotiate with their employers as a group, through a process called **collective bargaining**.

It is unlikely that individual employers approached the government to support the 90-day Bill legislation. In order to promote their ideas collectively, as a united body, employers have formed their own associations such as the Otago Chamber of Commerce or the Employer's and Manufacturer's Association (EMA). We will consider their role in the bargaining process.

Senior Business Studies   ISBN 9780170215732

The role of the trade union

Traditionally, union activity has focused on fair pay, conditions at work, the protection of worker rights, and ensuring that employers met their responsibilities.

The New Zealand Council of Trade Unions (NZCTU) has declared that wage and salary earners, and the unions, which represent them, have certain basic rights, which are recognised in international declarations:

1. The right to useful employment, to social security, to social justice, human rights and equal opportunity.

2. The right to organise and to form and join trade unions.

3. The right to bargain collectively with the employer.

4. The right to strike and take industrial action.

A stated goal of the New Zealand trade union movement is to improve the lives of working people and their families.

Unions today

In 2011, given the changing external environment and the onset of globalisation, the trade union movement's role has shifted from confrontation to conciliation. We shall see in the case study on Telecom (see pages 184-185) that the company consulted with the trade union before the decision to relocate the call centre to the Philippines was made, in an attempt to minimise the inevitable frustration.

Trade unions now are likely to try and support affected workers, or offer advice and counselling services when, for instance, a large business finds that they are no longer sustainable. Strike action is usually considered as a last resort option.

CASE STUDY

More workers made redundant

Up to 45 of the about 150 workers at Yarrows Bakery – one of the nation's last big independent bread bakers – are to be made redundant.

Earlier, KiwiRail announced plans to lay off 40 of the 172 workers at its Dunedin engineering workshop – one of the biggest employers in the city.

The Yarrows Bakery, based in Manaia, has been in and out of financial trouble for much of the last two years.

In February 2011, the company announced 40 redundancies were necessary to keep the business competitive

A similar review had taken place in November 2009 during which 28

ISBN 9780170215732

workers got the axe with a similar number taking voluntary redundancy just a few months later.

The redundancies came from all departments including management.

Meanwhile, KiwiRail chief executive Jim Quinn said the job losses 'had been a very difficult decision.'

'Due to a reduction in work at Hillside Workshops a staff reduction proposal has been announced for this site with consultation beginning today,' Quinn said.

'We know this is difficult for our staff and we will be ensuring they have full access to the consultation process and any support services they require.'

The role of employer associations

The purpose of a specific employer association will depend on several factors including:

• The size of the industry and the number of members.

• The current political climate including new government legislation.

• Changes in social trends or in fact any of the STEEPLE factors.

Consider the mission statement below which provides one good example of the role of one of New Zealand's largest employer associations.

Our mission statement

We are a membership organisation that promotes the success of business by seeking to create the most desirable environment for business and adding value through representation, knowledge and support.

The Employer's and Manufacturer's Association (EMA) Northern Inc has a key role in supporting its member organisations in growing and developing their business.

This is achieved through services such as:

• Employment relations advice.

• Occupational and workplace safety advice and training.

• Skills training and education courses.

• Publications, media statements, submissions on proposed legislation and occasional campaigns such as Fix Auckland to improve the environment in which to do business

Senior Business Studies   ISBN 9780170215732

Review

- Identify the chief reason why both firms in the first case study are going to make a number of workers redundant.

- Explain why in both cases the unions involved decided not to strike.

- Explain the role of a trade union in New Zealand.

- What is industrial action?

- Despite negotiations and discussions, explain why trade unions may still ask their members to vote on taking industrial action.

Thinking

- Why is strike action considered to be the 'last resort' option for trade unions?

- Having read the mission statement from the EMA website, what do you think is the most important role of this organisation?

- What are the costs to the EMA from a union taking industrial action?

- Explain how trade unions and the EMA could work together to resolve disputes rather than taking industrial action.

Research

- Find out at least three types of industrial action a union decided to take. What was the outcome? (You may wish to look at the Teachers' PPTA dispute of 2010.)

- Contact your local Chamber of Commerce and ask if one its members could come to speak at your school.

Globalisation

27

The global marketplace simultaneously creates opportunities and threats for New Zealand business. Now that local and international businesses are becoming competitive, an increasing number of them are now able to trade, utilise production facilities and connect with new consumers all over the planet.

A recent debate in New Zealand around the cost and availability of an All Black's Rugby World Cup jersey has highlighted that, despite New Zealand's relative geographic isolation, we remain very much part of a global network.

This unit looks at globalisation and some of the reasons put forward for its importance in business decision-making. By looking at some recent examples of New Zealand businesses that have decided to take advantage of the opportunities globalisation creates, we can assess how successful they have been and see what challenges for stakeholders remain.

Definition

Globalisation is the growing integration, interdependence and general connectedness of the world through, technology labour mobility and capital transfer.

Senior Business Studies   ISBN 9780170215732

Reasons for the growth and spread of globalisation

There is no one particular reason why globalisation has seemingly spread so rapidly throughout the last 20 years. We can point to a number of issues that are typically raised by writers on the subject.

- A significant fall in the price of air travel along with an increase in the number of routes available with greater competition on each route.

- Governments openly trying to attract overseas businesses by use of tax incentives and generous relocation allowances.

- The increase and availability of international schools, allowing more families to settle in many destinations among new emerging markets.

- Dramatic falls in the cost of communication. The costs of a telephone call between the US and India, for example, fell by 80% between 2001 and 2003. The use of VOIP tools such as Skype has cut the cost of a videoconference or call to very low levels.

- The growth of power searches (Google), on-line collaboration tools (Wiki's), and of course social networking sites (Facebook) have lead to greater data and connectedness.

- The introduction of wireless technology, increasing mobile and personal communication opportunities in local, regional and global markets.

All businesses have to engage in global markets to some degree. In such a rapidly changing economic, political, social and technological environment, however, one is left with the impression that unless small and large business seize the opportunities available to them then, at best, significant profitable opportunities are being given up. At worst, small firms in particular may struggle to survive as their competitors take advantage.

Opportunities arising from global connections

We looked briefly at a SWOT analysis of Disney Corporation from the 1970s (see pages 76-77), when the company was re-assessing its position within its own market and looking for ways to create new opportunities to grow. By 2011 they:

- Became the World's Most Admired Company by *Fortune* magazine, with the number one global brand.

- Were the only entertainment company to feature in *Forbes* magazine's world most valuable brands top 50 lists.

- Opened a new theme park in Hong Kong (2006).

- Planned to open a new theme park in Shanghai by 2012 in a joint venture with the Chinese government.

- Had their best ever financial year with global movie success such as the *Prince of Persia*, *Alice in Wonderland*, *Iron Man 2* and *Toy Story 3*.

ISBN 9780170215732

Think global, act global

Disney has been in operation for over 80 years and has been able to develop significant relationships with its stakeholders in many parts of the world. It enjoys significant global brand loyalty.

New Zealand, by contrast, is small, and even its large businesses start off at a disadvantage, since their brand names may only be known at home or in Australia. (Ironically, the advertising promotional line 'World famous in New Zealand' was created to reflect this fact.)

Organisations such as New Zealand Trade and Enterprise (NZTE) and the Asia New Zealand Foundation have been trying to raise the brand value of New Zealand products, and promotes new New Zealand brands to consumers in other parts of the global market. This process is known as **international trading**.

CASE STUDY

A number of successful New Zealand entrepreneurs discussed their views in 'NZ firms embark on their OE' from the *Business Herald*. Using the extracts below, draw up a table identifying some of the challenges and opportunities that present themselves when a business decides to take advantage of new global trends in outsourcing or off shoring.

'50% of our manufacturing is done in China. It has gone well. We have 15% fewer staff in our Auckland plant but our production costs are 25% lower. We have access to the latest technology that could not be available in New Zealand.'

(*Peter Batchelor,* General Manager, Masport)

'The benefits of off shoring outweigh the headaches. We have more access to better technology and the networks we have created give us important market research on the latest fabrics, logos and design possibilities.

'It took one year to find a suitable production plant in Portugal and then when that deal fell through another year to find our current Chinese supplier. Our production runs are still small however and sometimes we feel that we are the last batch to be made. Good communication is vital.'

(*Scott Unsworth*, Founder and owner, Orca)

'In two years our costs fell by 20%. After 9/11, international travel for adventure holidays fell by 30%. We were left with little option but to move our manufacturing overseas. It was an incredibly hard decision because we had such a skilled and loyal staff here in New Zealand.

There are other downsides. It is no longer possible for designers to walk across to the production engineers to discuss and sort out problems. Paperwork has increased and factory space in our overseas partners has to be booked 6–12 months in advance requiring us to spend time and money making sure our sales forecasts are accurate.'

(*Bruce McIntyre,* Founder, MacPac)

Having looked at your table what conclusions can you draw?

Senior Business Studies   ISBN 9780170215732

Research

- Investigate other local companies (or businesses with a national significance), such as Fisher & Paykel, who have carried out large scale outsourcing of their manufacturing processes. Try to discover whether or not they consider outsourcing to have been a success.

Global trends and business success

In Unit 17 we saw how more businesses are outsourcing their manufacturing processes, as part of the **supply chain**, to countries where the labour costs can be significantly lower. Outsourcing as a strategy to ensure economic sustainability has continued even in the face of considerable resistance from stakeholders.

CASE STUDY

Telecom to move 250 more jobs overseas

Telecom is proposing to move about 250 contact centre positions from this country to the Philippines during the next 18 months.

The company said today that when the process was complete, it would have around 1600 contact centre positions in this country and 700 positions outsourced in Manila.

Telecom Retail chief executive Alan Gourdie said that due to the length of the timeframe involved the number of redundancies was expected to be 'very limited'.

The move followed almost a year of trials and research, which looked at the impact on customer experiences from moving several Telecom contact centres overseas.

The outcome is that Telecom is proposing to retain its largest contact centre operations, 123 and *123, in New Zealand, mainly in Hamilton, with the approximately 250 positions being moved from a range of other contact centres in this country.

'In the case of 123 the trial data did not show us the consistent performance we needed to see in order to be comfortable with a large-scale off shoring of that operation, in which a detailed knowledge of an extremely varied set of products and services is all-important,' Mr Gourde said.

'In other areas, where specific, technical knowledge was particularly important, offshore staff have delivered strong results for the New Zealand customers they dealt with.'

The proposal would see further moves of Telecom's broadband support helpdesk to its outsourced partners, where it had been found it was easy to recruit technically skilled staff.

Engineering, Printing and Manufacturing Union national secretary Andrew Little said the union represents about 20 workers affected by the move.

He said with New Zealand's economy heading into a 'difficult time', Telecom's decision is 'unfortunate.'

Mr Little said the country needs all the spending power it has and jobs moving offshore will not help.

He said there could be more businesses moving jobs overseas this year as they review their businesses practices and adapt to global trends in outsourcing.

Mr Gourdie acknowledged the past year had been a time of uncertainty for staff in Telecom's New Zealand-based call centres, particularly those at the Hamilton operation.

'We have communicated openly and regularly with staff throughout the trials. Feedback on the proposed structure will now be sought over the next two weeks, with a final contact centre structure to be confirmed by early March.'

February 2009

ACTIVITY

Review

- Why have Telecom decided to make the decision to outsource its call centre operations? Your answer will need to make reference to global trends.

- Why do you think Telecom decided to retain their Hamilton call centre and not move this over to the Philippines as well?

- Fully explain whether or not Telecom have considered the impact of its decision on all its direct stakeholders.

Research and Thinking

- The previous case study was written in 2009. Find out whether or not Telecom's decision to move its call centre to the Philippines was a success.

- Consider the growing importance of the 'global marketplace'. Why do you think that measuring business success has become more difficult?

ISBN 9780170215732

Senior Business Studies

Appendix A: Extended case studies

EXTENDED CASE STUDY >>>

Afterglo

Key concepts

- Entrepreneurship
- Stakeholders
- Communication
- Corporate social responsibility and ethical objectives

Use the case study material and your own knowledge to answer the questions that follow.

After-balls back on as company gets in on act

After-ball parties are being planned for several New Zealand schools by a company that approached students on the Internet – after their school principals turned down the offer to organise the functions.

It is understood specialised company Afterglo is organising after-balls for up to seven Auckland schools, including Epsom Girls Grammar, Mt Albert Grammar and Alfriston College in Manurewa.

Company director Cade Pellett said he approached several schools via email offering to organize legal and safe after-ball events but most simply ignored the email or replied saying they were not interested.

So Mr Pellett went to the students instead – contacting head prefects through Facebook. And the response was immediate, with students scurrying to organise their after-ball parties with the company.

ISBN 9780170215732

Senior Business Studies

'We've got four [after-balls] next month and about two to three the following month. They're done legally … Police will never endorse what we do, but they're happy that we're doing it this way.'

The after-ball parties – which have separate R18 rooms for those who are of age and wanting to drink – have been met with mixed reaction from principals.

Some have criticised the organised parties, saying it was irresponsible for a company such as Afterglo to do what it does. 'I think the after-ball industry is just encouraging students to drink illegally and I don't think it's a good thing at all.'

'As the principal of a girls' school, I'm particularly concerned for the safety of young women in those situations.'

However, a number of colleges have embraced the idea and is happy with students and parents organising an after-ball with Afterglo.

One Board of Trustee chairman said although the school did not officially organise the after-ball, senior staff were aware of the event and were happy with the way it was being organised. 'We support it, so far as it's legal. If it's not legal, we won't support it.'

He argued that it was better for the school to know that a safe and legal event was being organised rather than let underground events go ahead.

Mr Pellett said on his company's Facebook page that Afterglo set up last year and specialised in organising school after-ball parties.

'Afterglo was created in 2010 as a means to provide nightclub experiences for teenagers across the Auckland region, all within safe and controlled environments.'

Unlike most after-ball functions – many of which are held in secret unlicensed locations – those run by Afterglo are safe and out in the open, the company says. Previous venues are listed on the company's website.

Parents are invited and security officers are posted around the venue. An R18 restriction section is the only place where alcohol can be consumed and only students aged 18 or older are allowed to enter and they must have ID.

Mr Pellett said the company had met police and discussed how they could work to make the events safe and successful.

'Then police said as long as we have an R18 area and security officers guarding that area, then feel free to have an after-ball.'

Police and liquor authorities this month sent letters to principals asking them to tell parents and students that events where tickets are sold and alcohol is served to underage people is illegal.

An Auckland police spokeswoman said yesterday police had no issues around after ball parties and therefore would not be commenting.

May 2011

ISBN 9780170215732

Level 1

- Explain how Cade Pellett has acted like an entrepreneur with Afterglo, his business start-up.

- What is a stakeholder? Identify any stakeholder conflict in this case study.

- Identify any problems with communication in this case study.

- Explain the importance of using technology and social networking sites to help promote the business.

- Has Afterglo been successful in using technology?

- By carrying out a SWOT analysis, explain whether or not you think that Afterglo will become a sustainable business.

Level 2

- Explain how Afterglo could be considered socially responsible.

- Given the views of a number of stakeholders in this case study, discuss whether or not you think that Afterglo is acting ethically.

- Fully explain why collecting objective market research on school after-balls might be difficult for Afterglo.

- Conduct a STEEPLE analysis on the issues raised in this case study to decide whether or not you think that Afterglo has the potential to grow its business.

- Fully explain the costs and benefits of one growth strategy Afterglo could use.

EXTENDED CASE STUDY >>>

Whale Watch Kaikoura

WHALE WATCH®
KAIKOURA • NEW ZEALAND

This case study is appropriate for both Level 1 and 2 students, and is based on a New Zealand operation that has proven to be a world-leading example of business success that combines sustainability and social responsibility. The article has been adapted from *The Daily Telegraph*, a British newspaper, and is designed to review a number of Māori concepts in business that we have covered so far. Before attempting to answer the questions that follow, it may be helpful to conduct some Internet research into Whale Watch Kaikoura.

Key concepts

- Business enterprise
- Risk
- Mission and vision
- Sustainability

- Citizenship (social responsibility)
- Kaitiakitanga
- SWOT analysis

Whale-watching company wins Virgin Holidays Responsible Tourism award

A whale-watching company based in New Zealand was this week named overall winner of the Virgin Holidays Responsible Tourism Awards 2009.

'Listen up, everyone: a whale has been sighted on the starboard side. That's the right side of the vessel,' announces Manu, our Māori tour guide. 'When I give the signal, you can leave your seats. OK, now!'

ISBN 9780170215732

Ser— Business Studies

On Manu's command, 40 Belgian, Dutch, Korean, Chinese, Australian, German and British bodies hurl themselves on to the viewing decks of the catamaran *Te Ao Marama* for a glimpse of the world's largest toothed animal: the sperm whale.

A frenzy of camera shutters and a chorus of 'oohs' and 'aahs' accompany the whale's rather demure departure.

Framed against the backdrop of Kaikoura's snow-capped mountain range, an adult sperm whale lifting its tail out of the Pacific Ocean is a truly impressive and transfixing sight; an encounter with nature in its most monumental form.

Locating a sperm whale at sea is a delicate and highly skilled operation but one that Whale Watch Kaikoura – the overall winner of the Virgin Holidays Responsible Tourism Awards for 2009 has been perfecting over two decades.

'All of our founders made their living from the ocean,' says Kauahi Ngapora, chief operating officer of Whale Watch Kaikoura, 'so that sense of respect for our cultural values and the environment has been embedded from the very beginning.'

According to Ngapora, who began working on the boats at 15, 'responsible tourism' is not just a handy marketing tag for nature-based tourism in New Zealand, but increasingly represents a core set of values and enduring beliefs.

'The 100% Pure New Zealand advertising campaign is a promise, and a lot of tourism businesses are now starting to realise that. Each of us needs to do our part to ensure that promise is delivered.' Despite the company's incredible success – some 100,000 people, a third of them from Britain, take one of its tours each year – Whale Watch Kaikoura is constantly reviewing its environmental practices and doing everything it can to enhance the customer experience.

The company is upgrading its entire fleet at the cost of $NZ15 million (£6.6m) with quieter, even more fuel-efficient and whale-friendly boats. 'There's nothing wrong with our current vessels,' Ngapora says. 'But things don't stand still and we want to keep up with all of the available technology.'

Underpinning everything that the company does is the Māori concept of kaitiakitanga, or custodianship, which demands that each generation protects the environment – and its natural resources – for the one to come. Despite their tribal differences, the idea of kaitiaki is universal among Māori, from the Bay of Islands to Invercargill – and tightly adhered to. 'It's absolutely our responsibility to deliver for the next generation,' explains Marcus Solomon, the director of Kaikoura Whale Watch. 'That's just part of our cultural being.'

Senior Business Studies   ISBN 9780170215732

'Visitors are known as waewae tapu or "sacred feet",' says Maurice Manawatu, the founder of Māori Tours Kaikoura. 'Part of our belief is that your ancestors walk with you, so we are giving respect not only to you but your ancestors. That's why a Māori greeting can take so long – we have a lot of ancestors.'

Twenty-two years on, Whale Watch Kaikoura is the region's biggest employer, with a full-time staff of 77, a custom-built marina, a fleet of six purpose-built catamarans and an annual turnover of $NZ10m. The venture has also been a catalyst for social and economic revival in what was once a poor, neglected community. Cuts to public spending in the 80s hit the town hard, especially the Māori population, which relied largely on the railways for work. When those jobs began drying up, five prominent Māori families came up with the idea of starting a whale-watching company but were unable to secure funding from the banks. Instead, these accidental entrepreneurs mortgaged their own houses to fund the project – now one of the most successful non-profit, Māori-run co-operative projects in New Zealand.

'Honestly, we had no choice – it was about survival,' says Solomon, whose father was a founder. 'Our children were leaving school at 15, without jobs.' A great bear of a man, Solomon, 40, initially worked for nothing when he joined the company and is proud that Kaikoura has gone from being 'a pie stop on the way to the Picton ferry' to one of the country's foremost tourist destinations. 'But an operation like this can only work if you bring in the community,' he says. 'And there's no quick fix. You need a 10-year strategic plan because that's how long it takes.'

Apart from kick-starting the local economy, Whale Watch Kaikoura has spawned a host of other adventure tourism enterprises – such as swimming with dolphins and albatross-watching tours – and made Kaikoura (population 3500) a national model for sustainable living.

In 2004 it became the first town in the world to gain accreditation under the Green Globe scheme, conceived at the 1992 UN Earth Summit in Rio. It has since begun a number of environmental projects, including a radical pay-for-use rubbish scheme, which aims to eliminate household waste from the local landfill site within six years.

Kevin Cole, the manager of Trees for Travelers, says the beauty of the programme is that it allows tourists to do something tangible to help the environment, and maintain a relationship with Kaikoura. 'We leverage the guilt that the tourists might have about the tons of carbon they have produced in flying to New Zealand,' he says. 'Over the past four years we've planted 4000 trees. However, Kaikoura attracts more than a million tourists every season – so the potential is just massive.'

ISBN 9780170215732

Transforming a small, isolated and rather conservative fishing and farming community into a beacon of sustainability and green activism has not been easy. 'I have to say it took a while,' says Kevin Heays, the district's laid-back mayor. 'The waste management scheme got a few backs up. And there's still the odd niggle. But now our community Is unashamedly proud of what we do here – especially when speaking to outsiders.'

Heays says the biggest challenge facing Kaikoura is persuading the younger generation to return once they have completed their education and the 'big OE' (overseas experience). 'We believe that our young people have to go and see the world, but we want them to come back,' he says. 'And one of the best ways to get them back is to kick-start their careers here' Kaikoura's other big challenge is maintaining the health and numbers of its visiting sperm whales, a species once hunted in great numbers in these waters. Their bones decorate the public parks.

'In our culture we have a saying: kanohi ki te kanohi – face to face. My breath, your breath' said Marcus Solomon. 'A destination is more than just a place on the map, it's the people you meet there and the experiences you share. So tourism has a huge responsibility – its arms reach far and wide.'

ACTIVITY

Level 1

- Identify three reasons for the success of Whale Watch Kaikoura.

- Explain the importance of kaitiakitanga in determining Whale Watch Kaikoura's mission and vision.

- Identify and give examples how the following ideas can be applied to this case study:

  – Innovation.

  – Sustainability and the Triple Bottom Line in general.

Level 2

- Conduct a SWOT analysis of Whale Watch Kaikoura and explain in detail the opportunities and threats facing the company in the next ten years (assuming that the whales still continue to visit the region).

- From your SWOT analysis, suggest a new strategic plan if the external environment moves negatively against the company.

EXTENDED CASE STUDY ▶▶▶

The Internet and New Zealand business:
Opportunities and challenges for retailers

Key concepts

- Marketing mix, especially distribution and pricing
- Decision-making
- Sustainability
- Stakeholder conflict

- Global trends
- Entrepreneurship and the Internet
- Online retailing
- Business success

Use the case study material and your own knowledge to answer the questions that follow.

There is a big reason the high street retail chains are under pressure: the Internet.

The explosion of online retailing, and consumers' growing confidence in making online transactions, are changing the way in which people consume goods and services.

As a recent illustration of that trend, when the Westfield group opened its new mall in Sydney's Pitt St retail heart recently, online auction site eBay took out big ads in bus stops near the new mall saying, 'Browse it at Westfield, buy it brand new on eBay.'

'It was quite an aggressive move,' says Trade Me chief executive Jon Macdonald. 'It was effectively saying to consumers, "Go into the shops to work out what jeans size you are, or whatever, then go and buy them on eBay." It's an example of a more active extension of online into the traditional retail environment.'

And consumers are certainly taking up that challenge, Macdonald says. 'There's a clear ongoing structural shift where people are more inclined to research, and then transact, online.' McDonald's own company in New Zealand has been a key driver in this change. Trade Me is the country's biggest online retail store recently recording its 400 millionth auction.

Astonishingly rapid as the growth of online retailing has been (sufficient to almost kill off music stores such as the collapse of the Sounds music stores in

ISBN 9780170215732

Senior Business Studies

2007, and the closure of the Wellington branch of Real Groovy), the technological advances are still occurring fast.

Even the way consumers can compare products before making a purchase is changing. New software allows people standing in a shop to use their Smartphone to compare the best price on websites for what is in front of them. Consumers now have power to compare prices and businesses now have to be aware of 'price-transparency.'

This issue was given extra media attention recently with the launch of the new Rugby World Cup Jersey in New Zealand by Adidas. The jersey was initially retailing in NZ stores for $220NZ but some customers using online searches were soon able to find the same jersey available from the UK or USA at $100 less including airfreight.

Stakeholder concerns meant that New Zealand retailers such as Rebel Sport did reduce the price here, but Adidas in New Zealand, the shirt maker, continues to face a lot of criticism for their pricing policy.

Changes continue at a rapid pace. In a development likely to be sending a chill through the heart of bookstores. Trade Me has had an app made where you can point your phone at the barcode of a book – in a bookstore or anywhere else – and the app will tell you how much that book costs, new or used, on Trade Me.

'This is where improvements in devices – in this case smart phones – are increasing the reach and relevance of online from beyond the living room or your desk at work or wherever you might be,' says Macdonald.

'Fundamentally, human nature doesn't really change and nor do the key ways we interact, but technology just makes a lot of these things easier and more efficient, so it lowers the barrier to people either comparing or buying things further afield.'

The Trade Me app is just one-way in which New Zealands most sustainable online retailer is changing and embracing the opportunities that the Internet and mobile technology is bringing to business.

From its humble origins in Wellington, Sam Morgan created one of the most successful sustainable online businesses after the dotcom bust era of the late 1990's wiped out the fortunes of many a young entrepreneur. Morgan sold the business in 2006 for over $700 million and now works as a social entrepreneur and venture capitalist in business as diverse as Medicine and Innovation

The Internet has also provided a number of other entrepreneurs with opportunities to create new sustainable businesses which now like Trade Me have woven themselves into everyday life.

Consider the following start-ups, their founder, sales turnover and current market worth (value).*

Increasingly, retailers with a retail or high street presence are finding it necessary to have an online presence, either through their own website or one like Trade Me. Macdonald, who says 40% of items listed on Trade Me are new, admits that some of these sellers who used to have a physical outlet have since shut the door.

ISBN 9780170215732

Senior Business Studies

Name of company	Founding entrepreneur	Value, May 2011 ($US)	Sales turnover, 2010 ($US)	Description
LinkedIn	Reid Hoffman	11 bn	243 m	A professional website for business people to interact.
Groupon	Andrew Mason	15 bn	760 m	The source of discount vouchers for every product and service you can think of.
Zynga	Mark Pincus	10 bn	850 m	Producer of games such as Farmville for Facebook.
Facebook	Mark Zuckerberg	50 bn	2 bn	Not the first social networking site but the best. As of June 2011, one-tenth of the planet are members.
Twitter	Jack Dorsey	Information not available.	Information not available.	A chance to share your thoughts with the world in 140 characters or less.
Yelp	Jeremy Stoppleman	500 m	50 m	A social networking site allowing users to review local businesses and services.

The valuations of Internet companies are difficult to measure and can change dramatically. Five years ago Bebo and MySpace were considered to be the latest Internet sensation. With the rise of Facebook and Twitter and the introduction of Google plus these faded star companies are now estimated to be worth $10m and less than $50m respectively. Well below their valuations in 2008.

Some businesses however refuse to be beaten and continue to offer a physical presence to their customers as part of their marketing mix. They argue that some retail experiences are almost impossible to replicate online. Valerie Riley, general manager of Elizabeth Arden in New Zealand, says, 'If you want a new lipstick, a new eye shadow or foundation, you need to go to a beauty counter. You're not going to be able to buy it online unless it's a repeat purchase and you know the shade … The same with fragrance – you need to smell it, and to my knowledge, no one has come up with an app where you can smell the fragrance.'

She recently returned from the US where, she says, all the major department stores have websites. She predicts that within two years most of the big New Zealand retailers will have done the same, selling cosmetics online at retail prices, and catering especially to busy people making repeat purchases. However, she argues that the online experience is no substitute for physical customer service and argues that many niche markets could still be created.

ISBN 9780170215732

Senior Business Studies

ISBN 9780170215732

Review

- One key global trend has been the increase of online trading. Explain how this trend has affected the marketing mixes of companies offering goods and services, especially the pricing, promotion and place.

- Identify three reasons for the success of Trade Me in New Zealand.

- Discuss whether or not the existence of Trade Me is considered an opportunity or threat for new business start-ups in New Zealand.

- Explain why Sam Morgan is considered to be an excellent example of a Kiwi entrepreneur.

- Choose one of the Internet start-ups from the case study and explain why you think this business has been successful.

- Explain whether or not you think that, given the rapid changes in technology highlighted in the case, Facebook will be as successful as it is now in five years time.

- In 1999, Boo.com was considered to be the best Internet start-up of the decade. Find out what happened to the company.

Thinking

- What are the 7 P's? Why could the existence of the 7 P's help 'physical' retailers to be sustainable?

- Explain whether or not you think that service industries have a higher chance of survival in the global marketplace than businesses that sell physical goods or services.

- What is a niche market?

- How could the Internet lead to the creation of more niche markets and therefore business opportunities for New Zealand business in global markets? (Interested students could read *The Long Tail* by Chris Anderson for some answers.)

Research

- Find out the current value of Twitter and its sales turnover.

EXTENDED CASE STUDY ▶▶▶

Air New Zealand

Key concepts

- External environment
- Market segmentation
- Marketing strategy
- Citizenship
- Whanaungatanga

Use the case study material and your own knowledge to answer the questions that follow.

Bad things come in three to put airline in tough position but is there a way out?

Natural disasters and soaring fuel prices have conspired to give Air New Zealand two of its biggest challenges. A **profit** previously expected for the second half of the financial year is now predicted to be a loss, but chief executive Rob Fyfe is optimistic about 2012.

On March 10, Air NZ said it was increasing its domestic and international fares because of the rising cost of jet fuel, which during the previous month had risen from US\$114 (\$149) to US\$130 a barrel, adding nearly US\$10 million a month to costs.

After the earthquake in February struck Christchurch, the cost of providing low fares for passengers and freight out of the affected region was about \$10 million.

'You actually are driven by what is the right response in this situation in terms of our employees, passengers and the Christchurch community.'

Then, last month, Japan was struck by an earthquake 8000 times stronger than that of Christchurch and was followed by a devastating tsunami.

ISBN 9780170215732

Senior Business Studies

'The combination of those three events – we have not seen anything like this for 10 years.'

However, Air NZ has a strong **balance sheet** and one of the youngest fleets in the region, he says.

'The world has thrown some pretty challenging operating conditions at us but as long as we can adapt faster than our competitors to that environment then I actually have a very strong degree of confidence that we'll emerge from this in very good shape' He added that Air NZ was the 43rd or 44th largest airline in world.

'But if I look into our 2012 financial year I'm actually very optimistic,' he says.

New opportunities were emerging. The Rugby World Cup in New Zealand was expected to generate millions of dollars and the company has decided to try and launch a new air service – subject to approval from the Chinese Government – from Auckland to Guangzhou.

China is becoming a very important market for Air NZ, although significant **external constraints** remain in place. The airline has been awarded five possible flights into Shanghai and Beijing but faces significant competition from the local carriers

Furthermore, Air NZ is forbidden from flying within China so the potential for growth is limited in the next few years unless there is a significant change in Chinese policy on allocating flights. Other constraints remain such as the fact that Air NZ has to hire local staff through a government agency for which the airline has to pay a commission. Also it has been known that rules and regulations regarding government legislation on employment issues can change without notice.

Greg Edmonds, Air NZ's Regional General Manager (North Asia) based in Shanghai, has argued that although Air NZ is a new emerging airline and is just about breaking even on its Chinese routes to Shanghai, it is important to be competing in a market that has the potential to be very profitable.

Mr Edmonds added that the growing wealth of the Chinese middle to upper class is looking to take advantage of the opportunities having more disposable income brings.

Market research highlights that many wealthy Chinese families wish to travel to New Zealand given our image as a safe and green destination and our importantly cultural diversity and history.

'We anticipate that a number of **market segments** will develop aimed at the higher income segment. China Southern Airlines flies from Guangzhou (south of Shanghai) to Auckland for an economy fare of 6000RMB. We cannot compete with that low fare but we have identified from our local market research sources that there exists a niche market where wealthy families wishing to travel to New Zealand will pay considerably more than 14,000RMB. We need to focus on this segment and apply a suitable marketing plan to provide an appropriate level of customer service.'

Mr Edmonds believes that 'Air NZ in China' is a sustainable business model and the company will benefit from its continuing relationship with the Chinese authorities despite the constraints outlined earlier.

Senior Business Studies   ISBN 9780170215732

'With the New Zealand Government supporting China's entry into the World Trade Organization in 1997 and the fact that we were the first country to sign a bilateral trade agreement in 2008, we enjoy a healthy relationship which will provide further opportunities. The key to working with China is to start small, network and build relationships. The Chinese authorities believe strongly in the concept of **whanaungatanga**.'

July 2011

ACTIVITY

Activities

- Define the words in bold from the text.

- Carry out a PEST or STEEPLE analysis on the external factors influencing the decision of Air NZ to provide a new service from Auckland to Guangzhou.

- Explain the importance of whanaungatanga for Air NZ's success in China and more generally for new New Zealand businesses looking to develop operations in China.

- Illustrate from the case study how Air NZ has demonstrated citizenship towards the people of Christchurch.

- Explain how Air NZ will benefit financially from splitting their market into segments with different prices for airline seats.

- What other information would the CEO require before he makes the final decision to segment the market for airlines seats on this flight from Auckland to Shanghai into Business, Economy and Premier?

- Prepare and explain a marketing plan describing a marketing mix for the Auckland to Shanghai route (and vice versa) flight service. Assume that New Zealand wishes to target a new market segment at the higher income (Business and First Class) Chinese family wishing to travel to New Zealand. Your answer should include reference to the 4 P's or 7 P's.

Appendix B: Sample examination questions

External Achievement Standards 90837 and 90838 (Level 1)

Unit 2 and 8

- Identify two characteristics of an entrepreneur.
- Explain one reason why people start up their own businesses.
- State two disadvantages of starting up your own business.
- Discuss one key factor that you believe has contributed to the success of a named small business you have studied.

Unit 4 and 5

- Define the business term recession.
- State one effect of a recession on small businesses.
- Explain why an owner of a small business is more likely to invest in the business when the economy is coming out of recession.
- Discuss the impact that increasing consumer confidence might have on a named small business (less than 20 employees or with local or community significance) that you have studied.
- Outline one reason why similar businesses might freely choose to be located in the same area.
- Explain how the grouping of similar businesses together increases local competition for those businesses.
- Describe the benefits of local competition for customers.
- Discuss how a loss of market share to a local competitor can affect a small business you have studied.
- Identify two ways in which the law protects the health and safety of workers in a health studio.
- Explain one benefit to the business of improving safety conditions in the studio.
- Discuss one possible legal consequence for this business of not improving the safety conditions.

Unit 6

- Define the business term environmental sustainability and give one example relevant to a deep sea fishing company.
- Explain two effects that a fishing permit will have on this company.
- State one negative impact of the fishing permit on this company.
- Discuss a positive outcome for this deep sea fishing company of operating in an environmentally sustainable manner.

Senior Business Studies   ISBN 9780170215732

Unit 4 and 12

- Define the business term gross profit.
- Explain why investors find the final accounts useful when making investment decisions.
- Identify two groups other than investors who would be interested in the final accounts of a business.
- Discuss one effective action to improve the financial performance of a named small business. In your answer you should identify an effective action to improve financial performance and provide an example related to the named business.
- Explain how this action would improve the financial performance of the named business.
- Explain how this action could impact on one other area of the business.

Unit 10

- Describe the different purposes of short-term and long-term finance.
- Describe the business term bank loan.
- State one disadvantage of using a bank loan as a source of finance.
- Explain two factors that a business should consider before using an external source of finance.

Unit 15

- Outline two reasons why market research would be important for a small business.
- Explain the main difference between primary and secondary market research.
- Identify two examples of secondary research that a small business could use.
- Discuss one effective method of primary market research that a small business could use to bring new customers to a small business servicing cars. Your answer should include reference to a survey, focus group, interview or questionnaire, and the advantages of the chosen method. You should also explain the disadvantages of one of the other methods used.

Unit 17

- Define the business term job production.
- Explain the key difference between batch production and flow production, using suitable examples.
- State the method of production that a business would use to produce goods for a special event.
- Discuss the method of production that would be the most suitable for a jam company producing its popular Apricot and Strawberry jam. In your answer you should state whether job, batch or flow production would be the most suitable method, give two advantages of the chosen method and two disadvantages of one of the other methods.

Unit 21

- State one reason why a manager would need to communicate with a worker.
- Explain one advantage and one disadvantage of using a letter as a method of communication with a worker.
- State one stakeholder that a business would need to communicate externally with.
- Discuss the impact of internal communication on a named small business. In your answer you should define the term internal communication and provide an example of how it would be used.

ISBN 9780170215732

- Explain why good internal communication is important.
- Explain how poor communication could create a problem for the named business.

Unit 25

- Identify two responsibilities of an employer that relate to local workers.
- Explain how a small business would benefit from carrying out one of the responsibilities you identified.
- Other than punctuality, state one responsibility that a small company could expect its workers to meet.
- Discuss one issue that might arise for a business due to an individual worker failing to meet their responsibility to turn up on time.

Unit 27

- Define the business term international trading.
- Identify one opportunity for New Zealand businesses that would occur as a result of increased trade with Asia.
- Explain one threat to small New Zealand businesses as trade with Asia increases.
- Discuss one barrier a small business that you have studied could experience if it traded with a business in another country. In your answer you should:
  - Explain how the named business could overcome the barrier.
  - Explain one possible consequence for the named business of not overcoming the barrier.

External Achievement Standards 90843 and 90844 (Level 2)

Some of the questions below refer to fictitious companies for assessment purposes only. One is a large construction company called Fast Up, which has a relaxed organisational culture, and around 1200 employees spread over a number of New Zealand centres. Other questions refer to Epic Airlines, a large airline that provides services to smaller towns and islands throughout the country.

Unit 2 and 5

- Explain one area other than self-check in that may benefit Epic Airlines if its uses new technology.
- Fully explain the difference between invention and innovation. In your answer you should refer to:
  - Research.
  - Product development.
  - Investment.
- With reference to a named business you have studied, discuss the impact on a large business of using new technology to export products. In your answer you should:
  - Explain one way new technology could help the named business to export new products.
  - Explain the disadvantages the new technology could have for the workers and managers of the named business.
  - Justify, with reasons, the use of new technology in the named business.

ISBN 9780170215732

Unit 7

- Explain one example that might indicate Epic Airlines is behaving ethically.
- Fully explain how Epic Airlines business ethics might influence business decisions. In your answer you should refer to:
  - Employees.
  - Customers.
  - The environment.
- With reference to a named business you have studied, discuss the effects that behaving ethically will have on the named business.
- Fully explain why consumers are more likely to use the named business if the business engages in ethical behaviour.
- Justify with reference to the negative effect(s) and consequence(s) for recruitment and retention of staff, the ethical behaviour in the named business.

Unit 18

- Explain one reason why the construction company featured above may want to grow.
- Fully explain the difference between internal and external growth. In your answer you should refer to:
  - Acquisition.
  - Innovation.
  - Growth.
- Discuss the problems which might occur if this construction company were to grow too quickly.
- Fully explain how this company could respond to overcome this problem.

Unit 19

- Explain the business term organisational structure.
- Fully explain the differences between a tall and a flat organisation structure. In your answer you should refer to:
  - Control.
  - Decision-making.
  - Communication.
- Discuss which type of organisational structure would be suitable for a large construction company with many centres across New Zealand.
- Fully explain the advantages and disadvantages of the organisational structure chosen.

Unit 20

- Explain one function a manager at Fast Up may be expected to fulfil.
- Fully explain the difference between being a manager and being a leader. In your answer you should refer to:
  - Roles.
  - Characteristics.
  - Styles.
- Discuss the impact of good management on a large business you have studied.
- In your answer you should explain one example of good management in the named business.
- Fully explain the effect of good management on employees and customers of the named business.

ISBN 9780170215732

Senior Business Studies

- Justify with reasons why good management is important in the long-term for the named business.

Unit 23

- Explain one way in which Fast Up could communicate their organisational culture to new staff.
- Fully explain why changing the organisational culture of a business can be difficult. In your answer you should refer to:
  - Company vision.
  - Staff resistance.
  - Communication.
- Discuss the benefits of a strong organisational culture for a large business (more than 20 employees and/or with a regional or national significance) you have studied. In your answer you should:
  - Explain one reason why the organisational culture is successful in the named business.
  - Fully explain how this culture could affect decision-making in the named business.
  - Justify, with reasons, why a strong organisational culture is important for a named business.

Unit 26

- Explain the business term trade union.
- Fully explain the role of a trade union. In your answer you should refer to:
  - Representative body.
  - Collective bargaining.
  - Industrial relations.
- Discuss the impact of industrial action resulting from a conflict between management and the trade union. In your answer you should:
  - Explain one impact of industrial action on Epic Airlines.
  - Fully explain how this could affect Epic Airlines customers.
  - Justify with reasons, a response Epic Airlines could take to prevent the industrial action.

Unit 27

- Explain one reason why Epic Airlines needs to be aware of global trends.
- Fully explain how the global market has increased competition for some businesses. In your answer you should refer to:
  - E-commerce.
  - Deregulation.
  - Foreign competition.
- Discuss the impact of Epic Airlines decision not to follow global trends and introduce extra services as part of their business. In your answer you should:
  - Explain one impact of this decision on Epic Airlines.
  - Fully explain the long-term effects this may have on Epic Airlines.
  - Justify, with reasons, why this decision may be appropriate for Epic Airlines.

Glossary

Aim The longer term view/target of a business.

Authority The responsibility to control business departments and decisions.

Breakeven When total sales revenue of a business exactly equals total costs.

Budget A financial target or prediction of revenue and expenses over a given time period.

Business An organisation that combines human, physical and financial resources to produce goods or services that respond to and satisfy customer needs.

Business success A subjective measure of the value, effectiveness or performance of a business for its stakeholders. Depends on the state of the external environment in which the business operates.

Capital Can be both fixed, working and share. Fixed capital is used to invest in fixed assets of the business and working capital is used to make fixed assets more productive by providing funds to help with the day to day running of the business to purchase raw materials and pay for overheads. Working capital is calculated by current assets minus current liabilities. Share capital includes the funds from the owner of the enterprise used to create the business.

Corporate social responsibility (CSR) Businesses that commit to ethical economic development practices.

Citizenship In a business sense, citizenship refers to a business acting ethically and responsibly towards its stakeholder community

Collective bargaining Negotiating as a group or an association.

Current asset Resources used in the short-term, such as raw materials to produce stock or funds to pay wages and suppliers financed by working capital.

Debt financing Borrowing funds for the business from a bank.

Desk research See secondary research.

Economies of scale When increasing the amount of inputs (raw materials) reduces the cost per unit of output (product), a diseconomy of scale occurs when the growth of a business results in increased costs per unit of its output.

Employment right An entitlement that is granted to the worker when taking a job.

Employer responsibility An employer's obligation to their employee.

Enterprise Any activity or project that a business or individual undertakes.

External environment Influencing factors that surround the business; social, technological, economic, environmental, political, legal, ethical (STEEPLE). These are outside of the control of the business but can provide both opportunities and threats.

External stakeholder Suppliers, customers, competitors, the local community or iwi, regional and national government and financial institutions of the business.

Field research See primary research.

Fixed asset equipment owned by the business, such as the premises, machinery or vehicles which the business will hold for a least one year or much longer financed by fixed capital.

Focus group A target market of consumers used to discuss a company's performance, a brand's reputation and/or to trial new products.

Franchise An agreement between the owners of an idea and those businesses that trade under this brand.

Globalisation The growing integration, interdependence and general connectedness of world markets.

Innovation The successful commercialisation of an invention. It has been sold in the market place.

Intellectual property See invention.

Internal stakeholder Employees, shareholders, senior managers, partners or owners of the business.

International trading A process of promoting domestic brands to consumers in other parts of the global market.

Invention The creation of a new idea, product or service.

Kaitiakitanga The responsibility of protecting natural resources for future generations.

Liabilities Debts which are owed by the business which can either be current (less than one year) or long term such as loans.

Levels of hierarchy The number of layers of formal authority within a business.

Sonic Business Studies   ISBN 9780170215732

Logistics process See supply chain.

Marketing A process of identifying and satisfying consumer wants and needs. The '4Ps of marketing' are product, price, place and promotion.

Marketing approach How a business prices, promotes, sells and distributes its product.

Marketing segment An identifiable subgroup of consumers within a larger market that can be targeted by market research.

Merger When two or more companies agree to join together and trade as a single new company.

Needs Goods and services that are essential to sustain life.

Objective A specific outcome(s), often expressed in financial terms, that a business wishes to achieve. An objective expressed in a mission statement indicates the reason for the enterprise's exsitence.

Off shoring When a subcontracted business's activities occur (are outsourced) outside the country of origin.

Opportunity cost The cost of foregoing the next best alternative.

Organisational chart A diagram showing the lines of authority and levels of hierarchy within a business.

Organisational culture The attitudes, beliefs, experiences and values that underpin the working relationships between internal and external stakeholders.

Organisational structure The horizontal or vertical configuration of management components in a business.

Outsourcing When a business subcontracts or uses independent agents rather than undertake an activity itself.

Patent Gives an inventor or firm the exclusive right to produce and/or sell the product. A patent is designed to protect intellectual property given the opportunity costs of research and development.

Primary research Gathering first hand or new data that is related to business operations.

Primary sector Industries in the primary sector such as agriculture, farming. Extracting resources from their natural habitats.

Production process Organisation of resources to manufacture goods and services to satisfy customer needs and wants. The three most common processes are job, batch and flow.

Profit Total sales or revenue of a business less the total costs.

Profit satisficing When a business decides to maintain a particular level of size or profitability.

Pūtuke The reason(s) for the business.

Rangatiratanga Chieftainship or leading a group of people.

Recruitment The process that turns a business's need for a new employee into a successful appointment.

Sampling Choosing the most appropriate technique and group of consumers (cluster, quota or random) to target when undertaking market research on a business.

Secondary research Collecting business information from previously published sources.

Secondary sector The part of the economy responsible for construction and manufacturing.

SME Small to medium-sized business.

Social entrepreneur The purpose of their enterprise is to create positive benefits for stakeholders as a whole and to act as a good corporate citizen.

Social responsibility See citizenship.

Span of control The number of workers or subordinates who are under the control of a manager.

Stakeholder Any individual or group who is interested in or directly affected by the activities of a business.

Supply chain The sequence of primary, secondary and tertiary business activities required to turn raw materials into a product or service for a consumer to purchase. The Supply chain includes both physical and communication flows between these different activities.

Sustainability Meeting needs of the present day without compromising the ability of future generations to meet their needs.

SWOT A method of analysis that examines the Strengths, Weaknesses, Opportunities and Threats of a business.

Takeover An 'involuntary' absorption of one business by another business.

Tertiary Sector The service sector of an economy.

Tikanga Values, custom.

Tūranga Position of the business.

Variance A variance is created if an actual figure for a cost or revenue item is different from that budgeted.

Wants Goods and services that add value to the lives of consumers but are not essential to sustain life.

Whanaungatanga Relationship, community.

Index

Titles of publications, broadcasts and films are in *italics*; honorifics, abbreviations and dates of publication are in (brackets).

ISBN 9780170215732

Senior Business Studies

ISBN 9780170215732

Senior Business Studies